Edward T Gastineau

A Hobble Through the Channel Islands in 1858

Edward T Gastineau

A Hobble Through the Channel Islands in 1858

ISBN/EAN: 9783744725521

Printed in Europe, USA, Canada, Australia, Japan

Cover: Foto ©Andreas Hilbeck / pixelio.de

More available books at **www.hansebooks.com**

A HOBBLE

through the

CHANNEL ISLANDS

IN 1858;

OR, THE SEEINGS, DOINGS AND MUSINGS

OF ONE

TOM HOBBLER,

DURING A FOUR MONTHS' RESIDENCE IN THOSE PARTS.

BY

EDWARD T. GASTINEAU.

WITH A VIEW OF BOULEY BAY, DRAWN FROM A ROUGH SKETCH
BY TOM HOBBLER.

LONDON:
CHARLES WESTERTON,
Publisher,
20, ST. GEORGE'S PLACE,
HYDE PARK CORNER.
1860.

DEDICATION.

To the reader, these pages are most respectfully dedicated.

In all humbleness of mind, I had intended dedicating them to *myself*, thinking that *I* should most probably be their only reader. But on mature consideration, I have come to the conclusion, perhaps an audacious one, that they may fall into the hands of some one else, in which case such a dedication would be considered both egotistical and conceited. Therefore, kind reader, whoever you may be, I have taken the liberty of dedicating this little work to you, trusting that should you consider it worth a moment's critical notice, you will not forget, in returning that most undoubted verdict, of guilty of writing a great deal of trash, to remember your usual kindly and generous feelings, and strongly recommend the Author to mercy, on account of its being his first offence.

THE AUTHOR.

June, 1860.

PREFACE.

"Travelling in youth is part of education," said the great Lord Bacon, and travelling in all stages of one's life, must also be a means of continued education.

Travelling is a very great luxury; not only highly instructive, but most amusing, and exceedingly pleasant to all beings intelligently constituted. It expands the ideas, which perhaps before have been woefully contracted; and it instructs the mind in a manner which books can never do, for many things that we read of, we cannot bring our minds to see in their proper light, without their actual visual confirmation. It also removes false prejudices, and overcomes many absurd scruples; and certainly to refined minds, is both most amusing and delightful. And not only so to the traveller himself, but it also renders him a very agreeable companion to others, always provided, however, that he is not much given to prosy descriptions, which it is to be feared is too often the case.

Now, travelling is particularly enjoyable when the tourist is in possession of good health. The case is, perhaps, a little different where the wanderer is in search of that health more than of pleasure; though even here, although the prostration of body from the effects of long sickness, must, of course, act to a certain extent upon the mind, still the mental powers are almost always sufficiently alive to acknowledge, with thankfulness, the delights that change of air, and change of scene must always afford, and more especially so when the invalid has the opportunity of finding those changes amidst some of Nature's richest beauties.

But it is not my intention to write an essay on travelling, a subject very much hackneyed, and though doubtless a most excellent theme, it is possible to have too much, even of a good thing.

Suffice it then, that in the spring of 1858, the subject of these sketches, was slowly recovering from a long, serious, and very painful illness, which had deprived him of his liberty for more than a year and a half, and had now left him in a shattered and crippled state; and having sought in vain for thorough restoration to health, in short visits to places not very far removed from London, such as the Kentish coast, and the Isle of Wight, now turned his thoughts to those beautiful islands of the British Channel, which lie closely adjoining to the coast of France, and are generally known as the Channel Islands.

It was not our traveller's first visit to these parts. He had been there on two previous occasions for a week or two, and was so charmed at those times, that he was determined to pay them a more lengthened visit, though somewhat against the wishes of his friends, who thought the journey one of too hazardous and fatiguing a character for an invalid.

But he did brave those dangers and fatigues, and resided in those charming islands for more than four months; and his idea is now to impart to any one who may be induced to read these pages, some of the amusement and instruction that he derived there, and also to record some of his thoughts and musings, on what he saw, heard, and was told, whilst resident in these beautiful islands of La Manche. At the same time, I distinctly wish to state, that it is not intended to write a guide book, which is frequently made only a medium for advertising, and is too often only a false representation of things; or a book of travels, which it certainly cannot be called, the journeyings being of too limited a character to bear that appellation; but only a kind of chit-chat description of all he saw, and what he thought, perfectly unshackled by, and free from all conventionalities. The Author may be perhaps allowed to add here, that these pages were not originally intended for public observation, but only for circulation among his own immediate friends. A combination of circumstances have, however, in a measure, compelled him to publish them, and he can only express his modest, but sincere desire that a kind and generous public may be induced to look friendly and pleasantly on his humble and unpretending effort, to bask in the sunshine of their favour and good will.

CONTENTS.

INTRODUCTORY CHAPTER.

The History and Geography of the Channel Islands. . 1

CHAPTER I.

ST. HELIERS AND ITS NEIGHBOURHOOD.

Hobbler's arrival in St. Heliers, and location there.—Description of the Town and its Environs.—St. Aubin's Bay.—Fort Regent. —The Piers.—Harbours.—An improvised race.—The Markets.— Elizabeth Castle and the Bridge of Death.—The Hermitage and the good old Saints.—Public Buildings.—Victoria College.—The People of St. Heliers.—A Review.—Sharp practice.—Telegraph Fêtes. — Regatta. — Hobbler's excursion into Fashionland. — Crinoline victorious. 15

CHAPTER II.

BOULEY BAY.

Hobbler at Bouley Bay.—Description of that Place and its Neighbourhood. — He studies men and manners.—Great variety of Characters in its Visitors.—Cockneys and their Peculiarities.— Sun-rise, Moon-rise.—Evening solitude.—Glorious Sea.—General Post Office and its machinery.—Gallant conduct of mine host.— Fleeting nature of travelling friendships. . . . 58

CHAPTER III.

GENERAL VIEW OF THE ISLAND OF JERSEY.

The size of the Island and general appearance.—How to see the Island.—Description of its beautiful bays, and charming coast scenery.—Its valleys, lanes, and roads.—Its orchards, flowers and beautiful cows.—Hobbler's ruminations on the scenery of Jersey.—The romance of man's life.—The people of Jersey.—Their Dress.—Their industry and penuriousness, and general character.—Their great prosperity and its causes.—Their Laws.—Society.—Lack of English Sports.—Clameur de Haro. . . 87

CHAPTER IV.

GUERNSEY.

St. Peter's Port.—The Landing and shouting porters.—Castle Cornet.—Harbours.—The Fish-market.—Churches.—Dearth of Public Buildings.—General View of the Island—Cobo Bay and "poor Billy."—Splendid scenery on the south-west coast.—Inhabitants of Guernsey.—Their Courtesy.—Their Gardens and Flowers.—Guernsey Society. 133

CHAPTER V.

THE ISLANDS OF SERK, HERM, JETHOU AND ALDERNEY, AND THE CASKET ROCKS.

Excursion to Serk.—The Voyage.—Neptune and Boreas at play, and the Steward at work.—Fair Venus in danger.—The parting glass.—Approach to the Island.—Harbour of Le Creux.—La Coupée and its story.—General description of the Island.—Herm and its tiny shells.—Melancholy incident.—Life and Death.—Jethou. — Alderney and its fortified works. — The Casket Rocks. 153

CHAPTER VI.

THREE MONTHS' RETIREMENT AT BOULEY.

Hobbler returned to his Jersey home, appears in a new character.—Cincinnatus.—My bed-room.—Our kitchen.—He studies domestic economy.—Turns cook, and goes a marketing.—A Thunderstorm.—The Fêtes at Cherbourg.—Hobbler's Dream of the Future.— Atlantic Telegraph. — The Comet.—Conclusion of the Season.—Harvest.—Fern Cutting.—Vraic Gathering—Florence Nightingale.—The Ladies of Bouley.—Adieu to Bouley. . 175

CHAPTER VII.

HOMEWARD BOUND.

Departure from Bouley.— Day-break.—Beautiful effects.—Adieu to Jersey.—A November day on board a Steamer.—Little episode on the Voyage.—Cupid and Uniforms.—The Guard's Story about the Livery.—Arrival at Southampton.—Hobbler on the Custom-house.—The Author's Adieu to the Reader. . 224

A HOBBLE

THROUGH

THE CHANNEL ISLANDS.

INTRODUCTORY CHAPTER.

The History and Geography of the Channel Islands.

BEFORE starting on his journey, our traveller thought it might be as well to read up something of the History and Geography of the Islands.

He did so, and behold the results of his readings.

When Mr. Thomas Hobbler was at school, some twenty years or so ago, he had been taught that the Islands of the British Channel were Jersey, Guernsey, Alderney and Sark; but now he finds added to them, in the maps of those parts, Herm and Jethou. Now where did these two new islands spring from all of a sudden? Perhaps they are only coral rocks, islands in process of formation raised from out the ocean, in a few short years, by those industrious insects? No, that cannot be. He finds that they are veritable islands, with veritable granite foundations; and, moreover, that they are inhabited and under cultivation. So he is obliged to come to the conclusion, that though the hydrographer, of thirty years ago, ignored their existence, they nevertheless have for many centuries past formed part of that family of iron bound isles, which stud the Southern British Channel, and which have so long been the terror of the navigator of those parts.

These islands all lie within one hundred miles of Old England, due south of the coast of Dorsetshire; Jersey being the furthest removed from it, and Alderney the nearest, the former being about one hundred miles off, and the latter about sixty. Guernsey is about twenty miles north of Jersey, and Serk, Herm and Jethou, within a few miles of the former, a little to the eastward.

They are all situated closely adjacent to the French coast. Alderney commands the harbour of Cherbourg, from which it is distant less than twenty miles, and Jersey is fifteen miles from the coast of Normandy. Jersey may be said to be situated within a bay of the coast of France, formed by Cape La Hogue on the north, and Cape de Carteret on the east, the former of which headlands seems to take Jersey, and the intervening rocks, within its embrace, as much as to say, nature made you part of our land, and you ought to come under the same rule as we.

Many people have supposed that these islands were at one time joined to the continent of Europe, but others again have laughed at this suggestion, though really there is nothing laughable in such a supposition.

Now I do not profess to be a geological scholar, and, therefore, lay no claim to a knowledge of that science; but yet it appears to me far from improbable, that one of those mighty convulsions of nature, which upheaved the vast plains of the earth, and formed them into those stupendous and cloud-capped mountain ranges that intersect this globe, and which levelled the hilly giants of remote ages, and laid their snow clad summits prostrate upon earth's surface, or buried them in the unfathomable depths of the ocean, I say it is far from improbable that such a convulsion of nature might in an instant have rent these fragments of our globe from the larger masses of the continent, and scattered them in tiny dottings on the bosom of the ocean. Or, perhaps, it might be, that one of these mighty heavings of the universe should in its convulsive throes have cast up these small lands from the depths of the great deep, where basking in the suns of centuries, they have reposed on its surface, and will continue thus reposing until another of nature's feverish pulsations, another age in the history of this globe, another breath of that Almighty power, which in an instant can again make this earth without form or void, shall once more change the crust of the world in which we dwell, and these islands shall be re-united to the mainland of Europe, or the ocean shall once more roll its majestic undulations over the spot, where once these small but aspiring specks of earth did adorn its surface, and where man, nature's greatest work, did once inhabit.

Reader, these were some of our hero's musings as he read up his geography ; and therefore I trust you will not hold me answerable for them, for you will find as you read on, that he is much given to musing, or dreaming, perhaps you will call it. As you will, and I am only too fearful that you will find his musings of rather too dreamy a character; but having undertaken to write an account of Hobbler in search of health in the Channel Islands, and to give his Sayings and Doings, and, as I fear, from the fact of his being an invalid, that the narrative will exhibit a great dearth of incident and adventure, I am necessarily compelled to give his musings in order to make anything like a book of it. I can, therefore, only beg of you, kind reader, to extract the good and the amusing, if you can find any, and throw away the bad, which latter, I very much dread, but sincerely hope not, will be the greater part of the affair.

What more shall I say of the geography of these islands? I think nothing at present, for as to the size and appearance of them, I shall treat in a general description of each island as I come to it; and, moreover, not having any intention of writing a geographical work, it is very necessary to be brief on the subject. I will, therefore, now proceed to give the result of Hobbler's historical studies regarding these ocean girt spots of earth.

Now he found in his readings, how in the glorious days of yore, one "Billy the Norman," took possession of the "tight little island" of England, and brought with him these pretty little Channel Islands as an appanage to the English crown, from which they have never since been separated.

He finds how, from that time they have been governed by a most charming code of Norman laws, upon which they may be said never to have improved, for the words reform and progress are held in abhorrence in these parts, and the laws of Jersey and Guernsey, like those of the Medes and Persians of old, are unchangeable.

And he also finds how La Belle France has often cast longing looks upon, and how she has often tried to get possession of these islands, but has failed in so doing; how her mouth has watered at the very thoughts of having them in her claws, and how that between the two great contending nations, the one having, holding, and possessing these presumed valuable lands; the other wishing to have, to hold, and possess them, the people of the Channel Islands have succeeded in getting the oyster, the two contending powers obtaining only the shells; the worst shell, perhaps, being that awarded to the party in possession.

The name of Jersey was formerly Cæscrea, probably named after the great Cæsar, who is presumed by some historians to have subjugated these islands to the Roman rule. The history of Jersey and the other islands, is but little known previous to the Norman conquest of England, and it will be sufficient to state here, that they belonged at that time to the Dukes of Normandy, and were attached by them, as has been said, to the British dominions.

I have also said that the French made many attempts to conquer these islands.

In the reign of King John, they made two landings in Jersey, but were speedily driven out on both occasions; and it is said, that that inert monarch was so impressed with the importance of preserving the islands to the English crown, that he hastened there in person, and after the enemy were repelled, he gave to the islanders their present code of laws. Another unsuccessful attempt was made upon Jersey in the reign of Edward I. Again in the reign of Edward III., they were defeated before Mount Orgueil, though, at the same time, they are stated to have succeeded in an attack upon Guernsey, which the excellent historian

(Falle) from whom I have gained my principal information, says they held for three years. This is the sore point with the Guernsey people, who stoutly deny the truth of the assertion. In the same reign, Du Guesclin, Constable of France, besciged Mount Orgueil Castle, the garrison of which agreed to capitulate on a certain day, unless relieved by succour from England in the meantime. The succour did arrive within the stated period, and the besciging army withdrew from the island.

During the reign of Henry IV., several descents were made upon Jersey, but though great devastations were committed, the same results always attended their efforts to subjugate it to the French rule. In the reign of Henry VI., that unfortunate sovereign who seemed to be alike the plaything of friend and foe, Margaret of Anjou offered to cede these islands to the French, in return for a certain amount of aid to be granted by them in reseating her then deposed husband on his throne. Baron de Maulevrier, by this convention, proceeded to take possession of Jersey, and obtained an entrance into Mount Orgueil Castle by the treachery of the Governor. The six adjacent parishes submitted to his rule with great reluctance, but the other six parishes of the island, under the leadership of Philip de Carteret, remained firm in their allegiance to the crown of England. For six years Jersey was thus divided, but in the reign of Edward IV. an attack was made upon Mount Orgueil by the English fleet, in conjunction with the forces under de Carteret, and the French garrison compelled to surrender.

The cause of Charles I., on the breaking out of the civil war in England, was maintained with great loyalty by the people of Jersey under Sir George de Carteret, and the Parliamentary navy were much annoyed by a squadron of ships fitted out by that officer. Guernsey took the side of the Parliament in this unhappy war, though Castle Cornet, a fortress of that island, manfully maintained the cause of the king.

Prince Charles took refuge in Jersey, and was well received by the people there, and remained in the island two months. He was proclaimed king in Jersey, when his unhappy father was executed; and returned to Jersey for a short period after that melancholy event, and was received again by the inhabitants with a kindness and loyalty of feeling he hardly deserved. Jersey and Guernsey were, however, both reduced to submission by the Parliamentary forces under General Haines and Admiral Blake; Sir George de Carteret having defended the former island to the last in the most gallant manner, retiring into Fort Elizabeth, and maintaining his resistance in that fortress until finding it commanded by the neighbouring heights, that succour was not to be expected from France, and that further resistance was perfectly useless, he submitted to an honorable capitulation. Castle Cornet was also not subdued until after a most gallant resistance.

In more recent times, during the reign of George III. when war was almost incessantly raging between England and France, three attempts were made by the French upon Jersey, the first two without success; but the third and last attack, led by the Marquis de Rullecourt, was of a more disastrous character, though the stout islanders, assisted by the British troops emerged from the final conflict with their perpetual assailants, as in every previous one, victorious.

The Marquis sailed from France with twelve hundred men, but only succeeded in landing seven hundred of them on some rocks between Gorey and St. Heliers. Under the cover of night, he marched upon the latter town, and surprised the Governor in his bed; and when the morning dawned, the inhabitants found the French troops in occupation of the market-place and Royal Square. The Governor, Major Corbet, under threats from the French commander of burning and sacking the town, in the event of any resistance being offered, sent orders to the Commandant of Elizabeth Castle, and all the officers in command of the different bodies of troops and militia in the island to lay down their arms, as resistance to the French forces, which the Marquis had represented to him as being over four thousand instead of a few hundreds, was not any longer to be thought of. The Commandant of Elizabeth Castle, as well as the other commanding officers, finding that Major Corbet was a prisoner, refused to obey his orders, and Major Pierson, putting himself at the head of all the forces of the island, led them against the enemy in the Royal Square, where after a very short conflict the French were compelled to surrender at discretion. This victory was not, however, achieved without a sad loss, for the gallant Pierson fell at the very first volley. Like a brave soldier, he lived firm in his devotion to his country, and like a noble one he died in the moment of victory, leaving behind him a name which will ever be remembered by the Jerseymen with feelings of the deepest gratitude and esteem. De Rullecourt also fell mortally wounded, and paid with his life for his temerity.

Thus terminated the last attack of the French upon the Channel islands.

The Governor has been accused of treachery, how far with truth it is not for me to say, though the most charitable must allow that he was a very weak-minded man, and quite unfit to fill the post he did.

He was tried by court-martial, and as may be naturally supposed, was superseded. There is little in the history of the other islands worth recording. Perhaps a romantic incident in the history of Serk is worth mentioning.

This island, at one time only a resort for pirates, was taken possession of by the French in the reign of Edward VI., but in the succeeding reign they were dispossessed by the Flemings in the following maner, said by Sir Walter Raleigh to be the chef-d'œuvre of stratagem. A Flemish vessel anchored off the coast, and requested permission to land, and bury the dead body of their captain in the consecrated ground of a chapel of great antiquity in the island. After some demur they were allowed to do so, on condition that they carried no arms with them, and on landing they had to submit to a most rigid search, not even a pocket knife being allowed to be brought on shore. On reaching the chapel, the Flemings shut the door. The coffin was then opened and the contents, a quantity of fire and other arms, and not the dead body of a man, were distributed among the men. The French were then attacked, and their number being very few, they were soon overpowered and compelled to submit to their clever assailants. After this, the island remained uninhabited until 1568, when it was ceded to Hilary de Carteret, by Royal Charter, and has remained for ever since under the dominion of England, and never again been subjected to any attack from a foreign power. Perhaps it were well, in closing this brief sketch of the history of the Channel islands, to notice the visit of the exellent and gracious sovereign of Great Britain, to those outlying provinces of her dominions, which took place in 1846, and was the last event of any importance in the history of these parts.

She was received by the authorities with much splendour, and with great manifestations of joy and loyalty by all classes, and her gracious and affable manners fully confirmed the stout islanders in their allegiance to their sovereign, and cemented more firmly than ever that bond of alliance betwixt them and the mother country which has now existed for 800 years.

May the visits of all constitutional sovereigns to the distant provinces of their empires always have the same happy and beneficent effect as that of Queen Victoria to the beautiful islands of La Manche in 1846.*

* Her Majesty has again visited these Islands since the above was written, viz: the summer of 1859, and was received in the same loyal and enthusiastic manner, and made the same favourable impression on the islanders by her condescension and affability as in 1846.

THE CHANNEL ISLANDS. 15

CHAPTER I.

ST. HELIERS AND ITS NEIGHBOURHOOD.

Hobbler's arrival in St. Heliers, and location there.—Description of the Town and its Environs.—St. Aubin's Bay.—Fort Regent. —The Piers.—Harbours.—An improvised race.—The Markets.— Elizabeth Castle and the Bridge of Death.—The Hermitage and the good old Saints.—Public Buildings.—Victoria College.—The People of St. Heliers.—A Review.—Sharp practice.—Telegraph Fêtes. — Regatta. — Hobbler's excursion into Fashionland. — Crinoline victorious.

" SOFT the wind blows and swift the stream flows," and her Majesty's Mail Packet Express steams gallantly out of Weymouth harbour, having on board Mr. Thomas Hobbler, who after having completed his preliminary readings, and packed up his traps, had reached the town of Weymouth on the previous evening, and now on a bright sunny morning in the month of June was standing on the deck of the aforesaid steamer, watching the receding shores of Old England, and singing to himself, "adieu, adieu my native shore!"

Reader, I will spare you the usual infliction of a detailed description of how he left London, and how he arrived at Weymouth; of the cabs and the trains, of the a.m's. and p.m's., and all the little et ceteras of a traveller's start, and take you at once on to the beautiful ocean. Under favouring gales, the Express sped on, soon leaving the shore far behind. The Island of Portland with its stone quarries and stupendous breakwater quickly faded from the view, and very soon the last vestiges of Albion's cliffs were entirely lost in the distance.

On and on steams the lively craft, the Caskets were breasted about noon day, and the islands of Guernsey, Alderney, Serk, Herm and Jethou were all passed early in the afternoon, and our traveller hove in sight of Jersey when the sun was yet high in the heavens. On approaching this island, he was struck as he had been on the previous occasions on which he had visited it, by the extraordinarily wild and rugged character of its shores. Rocks of red stone presenting quite a different appearance to the white chalk cliffs of Old England, stretching far out to sea, against which in stormy weather, the ocean beats with fearful violence, stand nature's mighty bulwarks to guard her coast from all foreign enemies, and render it, in rough weather, impregnable to foe, and unapproachable to friend. But on this occasion the temper of Old Neptune was unruffled, and our traveller rounded these rugged rocks in perfect calm, and was, without any adventure, safely deposited at St. Heliers, the capital of Jersey.

On landing at the pier of this town, one is subjected to a desperate nuisance, from the importunities and impositions of the porters, which it would be well for the authorities of the town to look to, though it is one that they seem to be quite indifferent about.

But the traveller is more than compensated for this drawback, by the complete absence of that still greater and most irritating source of annoyance to which he is subjected on landing at any of the continental ports, as well as those of Great Britain itself, viz. the Custom-house, to say nothing of the still more formidable passport system to which he is condemned on the continent. For this immunity from the Custom-house nuisance he is not however indebted to the States of Jersey, but rather to the government of England, which has conferred upon these islands such great commercial privileges that this system of espionage is not required.

Behold our traveller then comfortably ensconced in the town of St. Heliers, after being nearly knocked down the steps of the pier by the aforesaid importunate porters, and almost worked into a passion by their impositions, as well as those of the cab drivers.

Now cab fares, in Jersey, for a long distance are not immoderate, but when you have to pay two shillings for riding from one part of the town to another, perhaps not a mile distant, it is really too much.

The charge for porterage, too, which excited the ire of our traveller, was sixpence a package, for just handing them up the steps of the pier. But let these things pass, and let us hope that some day the States will think it worth their while to look into these matters.

Well, Hobbler has taken up his quarters at "Tozer's Hotel," in Bath Street, which was then kept by Mr. and Mrs. Kine, where he met with comfort, kindness, attention and good society.

There are many other hotels in the town of a most excellent character, such as the British, the Yacht, the Union, the York, &c., as well as first-rate boarding-houses. The living at his hotel was excellent and very economical, the practice being in Jersey, and, in fact, in all the islands to board you at so much per week or per diem, and not to charge for each item as they do in England. The prices vary from twenty-five to forty-two shillings per week. Now it is not my intention to give our traveller's diary to my readers, therefore I shall relate his sight-seeings and his doings during his stay at St. Heliers in a continuous whole, and not as the acts of particular days.

The day after his arrival, he proceeded to inspect the wonders of the place, and managed during his stay to see pretty well all the Lions of the town.

The result of his observations I will now record.

St. Aubin's Bay, in which the town of St. Heliers is situated, is considered the finest in the island, and is perhaps as charming, and as picturesque a scene as the eye could wish to dwell upon. It is compared by many to the Bay of Naples, but of the justness of such comparison Hobbler does not pretend to speak, never having visited that celebrated spot; but from all he has read and heard, he certainly thinks that the Jersey bay does not merit such a comparison. But comparisons are odious, so they say, and therefore without detracting from the merits of the Italian bay, it must be allowed that the Bay of St. Aubin's is one of nature's sweet dwelling places.

At the east of it stands the town of St. Heliers, with its capacious harbours and splendid piers, crowned by the fortified heights of Fort Regent.

At the western extremity of the bay is Noirmont Point, capped by a small tower; and lying considerably within the horse-shoe of the bay, at that end of it, is the town of St. Aubin's, from which the bay takes its name. It is deeply indented, the whole curve being six or seven miles long, though from point to point it is probably not much more than three miles. The coast line of the bay is backed by hills gently rising from the shore, whose slopes are luxuriantly clad with fields, orchards, and vineyards; dotted with villas, cottages and gardens, which form a most charming background to the picture. Nearly adjoining the shore at St. Aubin's is an old castle built on a rock;

and at the St. Heliers end of the bay is another castle, in a good state of preservation, also built upon a rock, and nearly a mile from the shore, called Elizabeth Castle. Both these castles are very picturesque objects for the foreground, which completes the picture of this justly celebrated bay.

The town of St. Heliers, commencing at the harbour which occupies the east end of the bay, has but little sea frontage, but extends far into the country northward and north-east. A walk through its streets does not very much prepossess the traveller in its favour.

The streets in the heart of the town are exceedingly narrow, and though many of the shops are of a handsome and extensive character, still a wanderer through St. Heliers cannot but be instantly struck by the almost total absence of anything in the shape of handsome public buildings. There has recently been a new bank erected in Broad Street, which gives hopes of a superior class of buildings taking the place of the ugly old structures now standing, whenever there may be an opportunity of rebuilding them.

There is a beautiful gothic building crowning

the hill to the east of the town, called Victoria College, and also an old Church in the Royal Square, and a new one in Bath Street. These are the principal buildings of the town; but as I shall have occasion to mention them again in detail, I will not describe them here. The newer parts of the town are a great improvement upon the old, the streets being much broader, and the houses of a superior class.

Fort Regent stands upon a very commanding hill or cliff, above the south-east corner of the town which it completely overhangs, and is perhaps the most conspicuous object in the whole island.

This fortress commands the town, the harbour, the roads, and the adjacent country in the direction of St. Clements. It was built in the reign of George III. during the regency of the Prince of Wales, as perhaps its name would lead one to infer. It was constructed at a most enormous cost to the British nation, the outlay being said to be over a million of money.

As to its utility, never having been tried, it is perhaps unfair to pronounce an opinion upon it; though it certainly did strike our traveller, that as far as concerns an exterior enemy, the rocks that stand all round that part of the coast in every direction, extending in many places miles out to sea, and leaving only a narrow channel as an entrance to the harbour, which channel being buoyed could easily, by the removal of the buoys, be rendered unnavigable, are a far greater defence to the island than the costly fortress. With regard to an internal foe, the case is perhaps different, and should the islanders ever prove refractory, doubtless this fort garrisoned by English troops could very soon reduce the town to ashes. Of course, the same remarks would apply to a foreign foe in possession of St. Heliers. But even these advantages can hardly compensate for such a prodigious outlay of British money, the addition of a million of money to the national debt, and a yearly drain of £30,000 on the revenue of that country.

Moreover, it has not yet been proved that Fort Regent is of any use at all against a foreign enemy, as it has been said by many that it could not be used against a foe at sea, for a volley fired from these heights would greatly endanger the safety of the town, as, being built on a quicksand, the houses would be liable to be shaken down by the concussion of the air, and if this be the case it would equally apply as regards its applicability against the town ; for if it could be demolished in this easy manner, it certainly does not need the building of a fortress of such costliness for such a purpose. Of course, these opinions are mere surmises, but this our traveller certainly can vouch for, as regards the foundations of the town, that every night as he lay in his bed, he experienced most sensibly the vibration of the house, caused by passing vehicles in the street; and the firing of the day-break gun at Elizabeth Castle, more than a mile off, caused such a concussion of the air as to have the same effect, giving a sort of rocking movement to the bed, which though very well for nurses and small children is not exactly the movement that the generality of people require to lull them to sleep.

To the eye of a casual observer, Fort Regent presents only a series of fortified heights. There is little to be seen, the works being principally underground.

These latter are, however, very strong, but without some interest only a small portion of them can be viewed by the public, and being of so modern a date, and consequently possessed with no historical associations, the non-military traveller will not take very much trouble to get a sight of them.

The harbours of St. Heliers are very capacious. The outer one is formed by two magnificent piers built of granite. One, the Albert Pier running out from the shore at St. Aubin's bay at right angles with it; the other called the Victoria Pier, jutting out from the easternmost point of the bay, immediately below Fort Regent. The distance from pier-head to pier-head is very little short of two miles.

The inner harbour is formed by a small pier on one side, and the shore on the other. The Albert Pier is a most superb piece of masonry, built entirely of stone, procured from quarries in the neighbourhood, and faced with enormous blocks of granite. It extends nearly three quarters of a mile in a straight line from the shore. It has a roadway capable of permitting three or four carriages to drive abreast, and an upper pier or promenade, where five or six people can walk side by side. The Victoria Pier is something similar to the Albert, though perhaps not so long.

The harbour is not accessible at all times of the tide, which is much to be regretted considering the magnitude of the works already executed; as for an hour or two both before and after low-water, vessels arriving off the harbour have to anchor in the roads, which in rough weather is not the most agreeable to the passengers, who have then to land in small boats. There is a vast amount of shipping enters this harbour, owing to the great facilities offered for trade by the commercial privileges conferred upon these islands, consequently the commerce is very great, and the number of vessels employed must be very large also. This makes St. Heliers' harbour both a very busy and very amusing scene.

Perhaps one of the most entertaining sights that takes place in St. Heliers, is that which was witnessed by Hobbler as he was one day lounging about on the Albert Pier. It is customary for the Mail Packets, when the tide serves, for them to come into the harbour, to put into the Victoria Pier, and for all the other steamers to go alongside the Albert Pier. Consequently, when the mail is expected, all the cabs and porters are gathered together in the former, as well as all the folks who have come to meet their friends, and a few of those who come to shew themselves. The boat is generally signalled, if the weather is clear, more than an hour before its arrival, and during that hour all is expectation.

On the occasion of which I speak, the captain of the packet, for some cause or other best known to himself, took it into his head to come into the Albert Pier, and though only a few yards from the end of one pier to another, the mouth of the harbour unfortunately lies between, and the distance by land, as I have before said, is nearly two miles.

The scene that took place on this occasion can be easily imagined by the reader. Immediately the intentions of the captain were clearly made out, there commenced a general shifting of quarters. The friends of those expected by the packet took to boats, as well as the porters, and were soon on the opposite side. But not so with the cabs. They all started off for the scene of operations, and those who had been nearest to the end of the Victoria Pier, were of course the furthest removed from the other one, and being anxious to regain their lost position, then and there they commenced a most exciting race. The only horse-racing of an authorised character which took place during our traveller's stay in Jersey was at Gorey; but as he did not see that one, he may be forgiven for dwelling a little on this race of cabs, as he is of opinion that an improvised race is better very often than one previously advertised, as decidedly in the former case there is no room for betting, or a chance of the best horse being the last in the race, because his owner loses more money by his success than by his failure. There were somewhere about twenty cabs, every man was urging his horse to do his best, and the whole course was plainly discernible from the spot where Hobbler stood, which was in fact quite equal to the Grandstand at a race-course. The pace was very good, considering the quality of the animals; the day was beautifully fine, the company rather select, and the ladies' dresses charming. Altogether the scene was one of a very lively and exciting character. Every body seemed in good humour, except perhaps the poor cabmen and their horses.

Now humane reader, do not think that our traveller was altogether blind to the fact, that perhaps cab horses were not the finest in the world for a race. He felt for them as, perhaps, you might feel—for he was very fond of dumb animals—but, nevertheless, he must confess that he was entertained by this extemporised performance, got up especially for the benefit of " Her Majesty's" liege subjects, by the captain of " Her Majesty's" mail packet the " Courier" on the pier named after " Her Majesty" in the royal harbour of St. Heliers, to which said captain he begs to tender his most grateful acknowledgments, as doubtless did many others present. And not only was the entertainment one of a rather rare and very racy character, but when it is considered that there is a complete dearth of amusement, not only in St. Heliers, but in the whole island, it must be allowed that this little incident was a decided boon. I might as well, perhaps, add that the race was well maintained to the end, the winners of course getting " the fares."

The markets of St. Heliers are rather of an attractive character. There is a large square market, with a covered arcade on three sides of it, for the sale of meat, fruit and flowers, as well as butter and eggs. This is a fashionable promenade, especially on Wednesdays and Saturdays, when it presents a very lively appearance, and the display of flowers is particularly beautiful.

People flock in on those days from all parts of

the country, and in the summer time, when the town is inundated with visitors, this market becomes a very busy scene. Saturday, however, is the great day here, though this market, as well as all the others, is very well stocked every day in the week. There is also a very handsome vegetable market, a fine large oblong building, completely roofed and lit up by sky-lights as well as from each end. This is where the flower shows are held. The fish market is something like the meat and fruit market, but of a very inferior size, and is but indifferently stocked, for there being no regular fishermen in Jersey, that is to say none who follow fishing as a trade, the fish generally being caught by small farmers, or men living on the coast, when they can find no particular employment on their land, the supply is most unequal, and the price of course the same. There is also a market for the sale of knick-knacks, hardware, shoes, &c., called the French market, and another for the sale of live stock.

These markets are all situated in the very heart of the town, of which they occupy a very considerable space, and are all contiguous to one another. Take them altogether, the markets of St. Heliers are hardly to be excelled by any in the United kingdom of Great Britain, and are not very often to be equalled.

The fruit market especially is well worth seeing; the general display of those luxuries being of a most choice and tempting character.

Elizabeth Castle is built on a rock, which is approachable by a natural causeway on the sand at low water, though distant a mile from the shore when the tide is up, and can then only be reached by a boat from the pier, from which it is distant, perhaps, a quarter of a mile. This castle, as its name would imply, was built in the reign of Queen Elizabeth, and is the place from which all the salutes are fired, Fort Regent never being used for that purpose. Though apparently of small dimensions, when viewed from the land, or the pier, it is really a very large fortress; the rocks on which it is built being nearly a mile in circumference. This range of buildings is far more picturesque than Fort Regent and far more interesting to the tourist, as it has been a place of some note in its day, and was once the seat of government. It was here that Sir George de Carteret held out against the Parliamentary forces;

and only capitulated at last on very honourable terms.

A walk across the natural causeway, from the shore to this castle, though rather a rough one, will repay the visitor for his trouble. This causeway is, however, very dangerous at certain times of the tide, and several soldiers have been drowned in attempting to cross it after dark, so that it has lately come to be called by the terrible name of the "Bridge of Death."

The Hermitage, or rather the remains of what was once supposed to be one, is situated on a rock a little beyond Elizabeth Castle, seawards. Here it is said that the good old priest St. Helier, from whom the town takes its name, was murdered by pirates some thousand years or so ago. These gentlemen are stated to have landed on this spot, in order to plunder the island, when the good old man thought fit to lecture them, and admonish them on their evil course of life, which admonition was taken as pirates usually take those kind of affairs, no matter from whom they come, or whatever their intentions, for they are no respecters of persons, and do not like to be talked to about their immoral practices; and so not liking his discourse, they killed the poor old fellow and the Church of Rome canonized him.

The story is a very pretty one, and I strongly advise my readers to peruse it. They will find it in most guide books. I would give it myself, but fear I should not do it properly, being somewhat sceptical on the subject of the history of these old worthies.

The Town Church is a building of no very great pretensions. It is an old fashioned structure covered with ivy, which gives it a very picturesque appearance. It has a large square tower, from the top of which they amuse themselves on holidays, with firing salutes from a small piece of cannon that they haul on to the roof for that purpose.

This church was built in 1341, and is interesting as containing a tablet to the memory of the gallant defender of Jersey in 1781, the brave Major Pierson.

There is a new church of quite a modern date in Bath Street, named St. Marks, which is a very pretty gothic edifice, and an ornament to the neighbourhood. There are several chapels in the town, but none of them have the slightest pretensions to architectural beauty, saving, perhaps the one in Halkett Place. There is also a fine stone building where those who have infringed, or supposed to have done so, the laws of their country are lodged, commonly called the jail. I say supposed to have infringed the laws, as the facilities for finding a comfortable dwelling there for any person to whom you may owe a grudge, are very great. This jail is situated in Gloucester Street, and from its numerous visitors, has been christened " the Gloucester Hotel."

Of the other features of St. Heliers in the building way, I shall not speak, with the exception of the College, which deserves more than a passing notice.

Victoria College is built on a hill at the east side of the town, and is a very beautiful structure, and from its very commanding situation, forms one of the most prominent as well as the most pleasing objects that the eye of the traveller can discover in this neighbourhood. This college was built to commemorate the visit of Queen Victoria to the island in 1846. The college grounds are very prettily laid out, and the walks and terraces therein form a very charming and shady promenade on a summer's evening.

And now I think all the principal objects of attraction have been passed under review. All these our traveller saw, which, of course, occupied a great deal of his time. As to the manner in which he spent his days generally, it was much the same as travellers in search of pleasure, or health, usually spend them, when " out of town," viz. in eating, drinking, lounging, talking and reading. In fact, in almost anything you like, but working. Of course, he went to market on market days, and on the pier when the mail packet arrived. He went to see a review of the Jersey Militia Artillery, on the sands between St. Heliers and St. Aubin's. He also saw a grand series of fêtes in honour of the opening of Electric Telegraph communication between the Channel Islands and Old England, and he was present at a grand regatta in St. Aubin's Bay.

Of the review, it is only necessary to say that the practice was excellent, and the bearing of the soldiers generally soldierlike; and doubtless should their abilities ever be called into play, they will prove a very efficient aid to the English troops who will have to fight side by side with them. This review took place under the inspection of General

Love, the late governor of the island, who together with the present governor, General Mundey, seemed very well satisfied with the proficiency of the men in their ball practice and general behaviour.

Indeed, as regards this said ball practice, some of the men were too proficient, or at any rate too confident of their skill, for during a temporary cessation of the firing, a man on horseback, probably thinking it was over, rode down to look at the target about a mile from the guns, when to the horror of all the lookers on, bang went one of them. The shot flew through the air, and was certainly well aimed, for it struck the sand close to the target, casting the dirt in a shower completely over the horseman, who was otherwise unhurt. This was doubtless very good firing, but it was also very reckless firing, and most assuredly very bad management. Either the man ought not to have been allowed to ride in that direction, or being there, it seemed running a shameful risk; indeed a kind of playing with human life to fire at that moment. William Tell and his bow and arrow achievement may be a very pretty episode in history, and especially so because there was an end to be gained by it; and all honour be to the memory of that brave champion of freedom; but of what earthly use it could possibly be to try an imitation of the exploits of the liberty loving Swiss with cannon balls, at a holiday show, it is difficult to conceive, and such an exhibition is much to be deprecated.

The Jerseymen are rather celebrated for close shaving in business, and I suppose they indulge in the same propensity when playing with gunpowder and iron shot. Certainly it was too close to be pleasant, and very sharp practice.

Of the establishment of instantaneous communication with the shores of Great Britain, it would be vain to attempt in a few words to enumerate the advantages, which must be very great, not only in a commercial point of view, but also in case of any rupture between the countries of England and France, a contingency it is most devoutly to be hoped that may never arise. The submarine wires start from the north-west point of Jersey, thence to Guernsey, from which island they are carried to Alderney which latter is in direct communication with Portland Isle close to Weymouth. Alderney being in sight of Cherbourg, any particular movement in the French fleet at that harbour would be instantly telegraphed to Weymouth; and in the course of a few minutes would be known at all the naval ports of England. As regards the fêtes in honour of the inauguration of this said telegraph, our traveller did not think much. They were made the occasion of a public holiday, and for the display of a good deal of party feeling. The first message was sent to the Queen of England, and an answer received back in a few hours from Her Majesty who was then at her seat at Balmoral in the north of Scotland. There were several processions, and a great deal of noise in the shape of bands of music, firing of cannon from the church tower, and pyrotechnic displays from the top of Gallows Hill, an eminence bearing that sweet name just outside the town.

These fêtes, however, must always be memorable in the annals of the Channel Islands; their object being to celebrate an event of such vast importance to the interests of all classes. The regatta was a very lively affair, but chiefly interesting to the visitor as giving him an opportunity of seeing all the beauty and fashion of the island at one glance. The rowing and sailing were very good, and the display of ladies dresses unexceptionable; crinoline being in the ascendant and having ample room for the display of its ample proportions.

In the neighbourhood of St. Heliers is some very good bathing at a spot near Fort Regent, called Point des Pas, a very pretty spot overhung by trees, and where the sea has hollowed out many cavities in the cliff, which form admirable dressing-rooms, at the same time many of the pools formed in the rocks make excellent baths for those who are afraid of the open sea. The bathing machines are in St. Clement's Bay more than a mile from the town.

Of the people of St. Heliers, as well as their manners and customs it is not my intention here to speak, as I shall have occasion to treat on these subjects in a general review of these matters, as relating to the people of the whole island.

Of the manners and customs of visitors to St. Heliers, principally composed of excursionists from London and its neighbourhood, it is only needful to say that they behaved themselves much as folks usually do at the English watering-places. That is, they fare sumptuously, lounge much, and promenade extensively; the grand aim appearing to be to enjoy themselves and to kill time. They like to see and be seen, and for this purpose are always to be found on the pier when the steam boats arrive, as well as in the evening when the town may be said to be given up to lounging and promenading, and in the markets on market days.

This, of course, only refers to the season when the varieties and excellencies of the wardrobe can be displayed to full advantage without fear of damage from foul weather. And this was peculiarly the case in the summer of 1858, when a shower of rain might be said to be the greatest novelty of the season. And so 1858 was a grand year in the annals of dress, which in that year displayed itself with a splendour and magnitude (at any rate so far as the ladies were concerned) unknown for many years past, and in no place did it figure in more brilliant hues, or assume more portly dimensions than in the capital of Jersey.

Now with regard to this dressing, there has been a great deal said of late, and perhaps more than enough, but as Hobbler likes to have a finger in the pie, and being at the time alluded to unhappily a lounging man, and withal not quite an unobservant one, he must have his say, and being of rather a wilful turn of mind, if he will rush to his fate by interfering in matters that he cannot possibly know anything about, I cannot prevent him. But I will at any rate decline to be accessory to his misdeeds by refusing to stand sponsor to them, though if he will talk on this subject I cannot hinder him, more especially as he professes to have taken at this time a short journey into Fashion's Dominions. Therefore washing my hands of the matter altogether, I will e'en let him tell his own tale, and get out of the scrape the best way he can.

Hobbler on Dress, and his Excursion into Fashionland, with his own description thereof.

Love of display in the article of dress must be allowed to be one of the great characteristics of the times in all ages, and is generally put down by stern moralists as a sign of degeneracy on the part of the people indulging in it.

No doubt that luxurious living, and luxurious dressing have often been the precursors of the downfall of nations. Witness the Romans previous to their country being inundated with Goths and Vandals, and all those gentlemen from the north who came so often, and in such large numbers to visit them. They were much given up to this kind of thing; and, consequently, easily fell under the dominion of their visitors, who had not yet learnt to doff their primitive habits and customs, and to don those of the more cultivated, but more enervated nations. But they did so in time, and they also degenerated. But your pardon, kind reader, I did not intend to indulge in an historical account of the rise and fall of fashionable empires. I think I was saying that dress was a great sign of the times. Well people did dress rather extensively in 1858; but let us hope that it does not foreshadow any evil days of degeneracy and ruin, but that rather it is only one of the freaks of the times, and that if it is carried to any particular excess just now, it will very soon, like water, find its own level.

Of the men folk at St. Heliers, I have very little to say. Suffice it that there were some of all sorts. Fops and dandies in a high state of starch and rigidity; men of business in ordinary costume, though much more free from conventional usages than they are in England, and the all-one-colour-summer-suited pleasure seeking traveller, which latter class formed by far the greater part of the community out of doors. The straw hat, cap or wide-awake, was generally the head gear, the old ugly chimney-pot shaped chapeau being almost discarded.

Of the ladies at St. Heliers, I would, if I dared, say a good deal. At any rate, I should like to say something, and yet I fear to come under the lash of their displeasure by some clumsy ill-turned remark; but—oh—yes—I must speak. And oh! be not angry, fair ladies, with one who would not for worlds offer you offence, and who now implores you, that if his muse, while sailing in such dangerous waters, should by any chance run aground on the shoals and quicksands of your displeasure, you will, with the clemency for which *the* sex is so *justly celebrated*, pardon his temerity, and pity the ignorance that dares him to steer in these mysterious regions. Before, however, entering those regions, it was necessary for me to procure a passport from the mighty ruler of those dominions, and thus I addressed her. " Oh, thou mighty and potent goddess of Fashion! condescend to grant to a poor man mortal the permission to visit your celebrated empire, if it is only for a flight across its confines; and, moreover, permit him to speak of what there he sees, and what there he hears; and if in treating of thy government and thy laws, he

should apparently violate in the smallest degree
the integrity of your dominions, believe it not, that
he has the remotest thought of disputing, or even
questioning the justice of your rule. No, he is
well convinced that you are far too firmly seated
on your throne, and your subjects too deeply rooted
in their adherence and allegiance to your sway,
and their affections too securely fixed upon you,
for any remarks that he, poor, vain mortal can
make, to have any effect; and, moreover, that no
act of his, or any of his species, could, by the
remotest possibility, affect the stability of your
power. Therefore, in all humility, soliciting your
indulgence, and craving your mercy, he bows
before your footstool, does homage to your power,
and asks permission to travel through your vast
dominions, promising, by putting a curb on his
thoughts, and a bridle on his pen, to take every
precaution against coming into collision with any
of your subjects." She heard, the mighty Goddess,
and with a scornful laugh granted the required
passport, and screwing up my courage, I entered
those strange lands, and woe is me the day I
did so.

Now the first of Fashion's favourites that I

encountered was Hat, the ruler appointed over a large territory, where she reigns with almost supreme authority, having driven out the former viceroy in these parts, one called Bonnet. Now to say the least of it, this Hat is a usurper, though it must be confessed that Bonnet was getting very old and effete, and during the last few years of power had but little hold on her subjects, and exercised over their heads but a very feeble sway; and her power, with the exception of sundry dashes made in desperation to regain her position, had always the appearance of a falling one, owing much of its support to another power, over which she exercised no authority, and with whom she ought not to have had any connection—one commonly called Shoulders. Hat, like the deities of heathen mythology, had the power of changing her form and appearance at pleasure. Sometimes she was gloomy and grand, completely overclouding the province over which she was supposed to rule with beneficence, and to which, as its head, she was supposed to be the ornament. At other times she assumed a plumed and war-like port, not quite compatible with the sweet, beautiful, and peaceful character of her dominions. At another time, she appeared in such questionable shape, and such diminutive size, that she was hardly visible; scarcely seeming to have any connection with her subjects, and certainly not fulfilling the duties for which she was destined.

But her disguises were too numerous for me to describe. Some of them were certainly very charming, especially when the subject upon whom she bestowed her favours, was revelling in the bright sunshine of youth and innocence, when the brow was unmarked by care, and the general aspect was blooming and feminine. Then was the rule of Hat, a charming rule, and imparted to the beautiful dominion of which she was the crown, much of the charming effect of which she was possessed herself. But some of them were also very hideous, and Hat exercised a tyrannical and far from beneficent rule over some of her subjects. Where the hey-day of youth was past, where the suns of many years had gone over their heads, and where nature had given them a hard and masculine exterior, then was Hat but an ugly tyrant, making its subjects or victims appear more ugly than itself .And, moreover, there was very little religion in this Hat. She seemed to have a particular antipathy to Sundays and churches, and strange to say always allowed poor deposed Bonnet to resume her sway in those places, and on those days. And as to morality, it used to be said in the days when Bonnet was sinking into insignificance, when the object of her authority was beginning to repudiate her rule, and she had to call in the aid of the aforesaid shoulders to keep her on her throne, that she held out a certain temptation for the perpetration of a certain little pleasantrie upon the aforesaid subjects, the said Bonnet being called in this case, " Kiss if you will." Now, this of course, was very improper, though I cannot help thinking, that if Bonnet was ever guilty of offering the temptation for the commission of such improprieties, by the forms she assumed, Hat was in many of her shapes, far more inviting for the perpetration of such offences. But I must proceed, Hat and I had a little pleasant conversation, and then we parted.

The next of Fashion's delegated rulers that I encountered was known as military heels. Military heels did not appear to reign with anything like the universal authority that Hat did. Nevertheless, he, I am sure it must be masculine gender, had obtained much sway over certain classes, who owed the more general sovereignty of Military heel's superior in command, Boot. I had not much to say to Military heels. I thought him a very clattering and independent sort of a fellow. He was not exactly inelegant, though I could not help thinking that he was not a ruler calculated to improve the development of the forms of his subjects.

I met many others of fashion's favourites of different kinds and of various colours. But I must pass them by, only remarking that her favourite colour seemed to be red, especially in that peculiar garment of which man used at one time hardly to dare to speak, but being now exposed for admiration, I suppose I may mention, namely the petticoat. There was also a fancy in some parts of Fashionland to indulge in a festooning or reefing process, not particularly elegant I must confess, but then I was told it was convenient, and that was enough. I now proceed to the last grand encounter. Though last not least, for this was by far the most formidable personage of the whole body, and I hardly know how to describe her, for I feel, like Bob Acres, the courage oozing out at my finger ends, and would almost like to shirk the description. But no, I cannot do so, for as I am now fairly in the very heart of Fashionland, and cannot, after permission obtained to travel there, retreat without ignominy; I will screw my courage to the sticking place, and most sincerely hope that I shall not fail.

The mighty personage who now crossed my path, was no less an one than the Lady Crinoline, the greatest, the grandest, and the most weighty of Fashion's favourites. This mighty amazon has encountered enemies innumerable, and of every character. Anger, spite, and ridicule have attacked her times out of number; but without the shadow of a chance of success. Vast and expansive in her proportions, ruler over immense dominions, over which she holds undivided sway, she emerges from every conflict, not only victorious, but spreads her ample folds with greater amplitude, and bears down with greater weight all opposition. Hear ye raging Paterfamilias! hear ye poor half crushed mortals! who encounter her in public thoroughfares, or in public vehicles! hear ye snarling, but sharped-toothed critics, who vent your impotent wrath upon her audacious head! proud and erect she dares you battle; against all

E

comers she boldly maintains her own, and laughs ye all to scorn.

Away then, vain man, and fight no longer against the power, which for the present seems invulnerable!

It has been said by my editor, that I saw no architecture of any pretensions in St. Heliers. This only alluded to the architecture of brick and stone, for the architecture of Crinoline is of marvellous pretensions, and on first seeing it exhibited at the Magazin des Modes, it struck me as the most wonderfully built fabric I had ever seen.

The only thing I could compare it to, was the Great Crystal Palace when in course of construction; for the intricacy of detail was so puzzling, that the eye was quite pained in trying to understand it.

But I will not attempt to describe Crinoline in its time of growing, its constructive period. I will not dare to enter further into the mysteries of that mysterious power, lest provoking the wrath of her Ladyship, and above all that of the great Goddess herself, I should be for ever condemned to walk this nether world imprisoned in one of those terrible cages, an awful warning of the punishment that awaits all who have the folly or temerity to brave their power. No, the recollection of an accidental collision I had with Lady Crinoline is sufficiently vivid in my memory to allow me ever to contemplate the idea of giving her a tangible cause of quarrel.

Generally speaking, no sooner did I descry a Crinoline in the distance approaching me—I crave your mercy, fair ladies, for speaking of Lady Crinoline to whom you give your allegiance, rather than of yourselves, for where the individual is short-sighted, the Crinoline comes into view long before the lady who shelters behind her bulwarks, a sort of avant-courrier—well, no sooner did I see a Crinoline approaching, than like a well-bred dog, I took to the middle of the road, or tried to hide my diminished head in some neighbouring shop, if so be another Crinoline had not already got possession of that retreat, in which case I was compelled to retire altogether. But in the instance I allude to, retreat was altogether cut off, and I had nothing left, but to stand and meet the shock, and bow with dignity to my inevitable fate. With bated breath, and an air of desperation, I planted my two assistant legs, I think my historian has stated that I am lame, as a kind of stockade, a little in advance on either side, and then quietly awaited my doom. Onward sweeps the moving tower, and now looms in the distance the hat that hides the face, that belongs to the fair being, whose heart beats underneath that vast press of muslin, hooping, tubing, and cordage. And while the gentle heart beneath that hard exterior pities that poor man, and wishes most sincerely that he was at home, or in heaven, or any where out of reach of the impending danger, stern Crinoline seems to say " avaunt thou poor thin thing! What doest thou here? There is no room for thee. Why darest thou, an unprotected male, to walk the narrow streets of this town? Art thou aweary of thy life, that thus thou dost court thy doom?" Onward, majestic, stately unrelenting, and resistless it sweeps... It comes... It comes...It is past.

And where was that poor mortal that had thus unhappily come into contact with the hard Lady Crinoline? Behold him, your humble servant I mean, spinning like a humming-top far down the street, scarcely able to maintain his equilibrium, and then as puffing, panting, and struggling for breath, he leans against the nearest support, he hears faintly, but clearly, the triumphant and ironical laugh of Crinoline, as she disappears in the distance, and thanks his stars that he has escaped perfect annihilation; but cannot help sighing for the palmy days of his health time, when by a series of flying leaps, he might have avoided the dangers of this perilous street navigation.

With wounded pride, and dejected spirits, I went to my home, and exhausted nature requiring recruitment, I thought I would dine. But even here Crinoline pursued me. One would have supposed that her triumph of the morning would have been sufficient. But no, with a lady on either side, I found myself so hooped in, that I began to fancy that I must have been transformed by the enraged Goddess into a tub—most assuredly I felt that I had become a butt—and that she had put iron hoops around me to keep me together, for which there might be some necessity, after my late encounter. And then I fancied that the dog was sitting on my feet. Now, reader, there really was a dog at the Hotel, very fond of sitting under the table at meal times, so pray do not think this all a chimera of my brain, disordered by the shock it had sustained. Well, I fancied the dog was sitting on my feet, but found it was only sundry coils of tubing belonging to a lady, my vis-à-vis. What a happiness that every day of trouble has an end, though it does not always follow that night brings relief. So with me, crushed and crest-fallen, I retired to my chamber, and having extinguished my candle, I admitted the soft beams of nature's silvery orb of night, and melting under its gentle influence, I fear me much that I became mooney; for my thoughts still running on Crinoline, I indulged in the following apostrophe.

" Oh, Crinoline, Crinoline! when wilt thou cease thy rule of despotism ? Thinkest thou that having, by the aid of the all powerful Goddess, so surrounded and hemmed in all thy subjects, or rather victims, thou wilt for ever retain their allegiance ?

" Oh no! not only will they some day refuse to bear the heavy yoke thou hast imposed upon them, but thy proud mistress, in one of her capricious moods, may altogether discard thee from her service. Be wise, therefore, in time ; and moderate thy pretensions, and then perhaps thy reign may be prolonged.

" And, oh, ye fair ones ! who do homage to this mighty Goddess, and bow before the footstool of her viceroy, Lady Crinoline ; how long will ye be content to bear this heavy burden; how long will ye submit to be bound with hoops of iron and strong cords. I appeal to ye all!

"Small children, who stagger beneath the weight imposed upon you by fashionable mothers. Young maidens, whose elegant forms are made to look like huge bells, or monstrous sugar loaves; matronly dames whose comely figures are so terribly disguised as scarcely to be recognisable; and venerable ladies whose staid carriage and time-honoured locks of silver should render thee the landmarks of respect and veneration, but who beneath this load of Fashion's fancy are made to imitate tripping damsels; to all of ye I appeal to shake off this mighty incubus, and compel the Lady Crinoline to moderate her demands upon you, or return at once to the far more beneficent, and elegant rule of the Flowing Robe."

A cloud shot athwart the midnight lamp of heaven, and I awoke from my dreaming, and with a cry of horror I sprang across the borders of Fashionland, happy to have escaped with sound limbs from such a perilous adventure, a repetition of which nothing should ever induce me to undertake.

Here ended Hobbler's account of his wonderful excursion. And right glad is the author of his travels that he has at last quitted such dangerous and slippery ground; and right glad will the reader be to find that his peregrinations, and the relation thereof have, at length, terminated. Besides he is probably rather too late in the field, as it is said that the Lady Crinoline is already beating a steady retreat, and his advice is useless; "The guard dies but never surrenders." So with Crinoline, it will doubtless retain its elasticity and portliness to the last, which last probably will not be very far off—Crinoline dies but never surrenders.

But why lingers our traveller so long among the narrow streets of St. Heliers, when the balmy breezes and brilliant sunshines of midsummer should woo him away to the beautiful country.

It is true that his days had been pleasantly spent in the town, for there he met many very agreeable companions from whom he experienced much kindness, and in whose society time rolled rapidly away. But he has now made up his mind to leave them and the town as well, and take up his abode at the hotel in the romantic Bay of Bouley, on the north side of the island. He has studied streets, buildings, promenades and fashions long enough, and now thinks it is time to betake him to the contemplation of nature, as displayed in the beautiful scenery of this island, and perhaps, also, as delineated in her master-piece, man, of whom and his manners he will doubtless have to speak in the next chapter.

So here we drop the curtain on our friend Hobbler as a townsman, for to a certain degree he was compelled to submit to town usages, but when it rises again, we shall find him al fresco, a countryman, a man at his perfect ease.

CHAPTER II.

BOULEY BAY.

Hobbler at Bouley Bay.—Description of that Place and its Neighbourhood.—He studies men and manners.—Great variety of Characters in its Visitors.—Cockneys and their Peculiarities.—Sun-rise, Moon-rise.—Evening solitude.—Glorious Sea.—General Post Office and its machinery.—Gallant conduct of mine host.—Fleeting nature of travelling friendships.

"God made the country, and man the town." So said one of our greatest poets, and so thought Hobbler as he quitted his town residence, and emerging into the country, exchanged the view of bricks and mortar, the sameness and monotony of which palls upon the vision, for the ever beautiful freshness of the open country.

One charming afternoon at the end of June, our traveller found himself deposited at the door of the hotel at Bouley Bay, after a very pleasant drive of five miles right across the island. This bay lies on the north coast facing Old England, but shut out from it by Cape La Hogue on the coast of France about twenty-five miles off, which Cape stretches out its long arm and completely overlaps this part of the island. The French coast stretches away in both directions opposite Bouley from Cape La Hogue to Cape Carteret at distances varying from twenty-five to fifteen miles. The bay is approachable by a zig-zag road between two hills cut in the face of one of them, and on descending this road, the traveller has one of the prettiest prospects spread out before him that he could possibly wish to behold, particularly if the day should be one of bright sunshine. Before and below him can be traced the road, picturesque in all its windings, the old fashioned hotel, with its red tiled roof, glittering in the sunbeams at the bottom. On his right hand are steep hills of an altitude of four or five hundred feet, covered with fern, and every here and there large masses of rock cropping out of their sides.

Carrying the eye beyond, these hills are succeeded by wild craggy cliffs stretching away in the distance and terminated by a curious point of rock, called the Tour de Rozel, which is kept whitewashed as a landmark, and presents a most singular appearance in the sunlight.

This rock forms the westernmost point of the bay. On the other side are almost perpendicular hills or crags, for they are principally composed of large masses of rock; in some places their sides covered with gorse and fern, and at others a beautiful vein of rich violet coloured clay peeping out; the whole crowned by frowning blocks of stone of an enormous size, which seem as if they had been placed there by some mighty giant's hand, and appear to maintain their position so slightly, that one is tempted to imagine that the smallest touch would send them bounding and crashing into the valley below. At one point of the road is a sweet little bit of sylvan scenery, quite away from the general character of that described above, and serves by its appearance of quiet repose to shew off to greater advantage the grandeur of the surrounding prospect.

The beautiful ocean lies in front, glittering in the sunshine, with the Echerons rocks sprinkled on its surface, at a distance of about seven miles from the shore; the coast of France fills in the extreme back ground.

The beauty of this prospect is one that cannot fail to arrest the eye of the traveller if he has any real love for the beauties of nature, and checking his downward course, he is lost in admiration and delight.

Descending to the house, the road turns sharp round to the left, running below a series of beetling cliffs, and finally terminates at the pier, which is built of stone, and projecting its one arm at right angles from the shore, forms the little harbour of Bouley. From the head of the pier, the hills assume a very bold and rugged character, rising to a great height, running away to the westward, and terminating in Green Rock Point.

The road and the pier were constructed at an enormous cost to the States of Jersey, with the idea of making a Harbour of Refuge here. But such an idea appears to have been abandoned long since, as many of the platforms for guns, and several batteries have fallen to decay, which were evidently intended to have formed the defences for the harbour. This bay is still very strong. There are two batteries remaining, one mounting two, and the other three guns of large size, and our traveller was informed, that in case of apprehended invasion, this bay and the heights surrounding it, would mount as many as seventy guns. This fact, together with the rocky and dangerous character of the coast, renders Bouley Bay all but impregnable to an open attack. The water here is very deep, and the shore being very precipitate, vessels of a large size can approach very close at all times of the tide, and this latter circumstance, as well as the fact that it would only require one pier to be built, render it very probable that the government of England will some day choose this bay for the construction of a Naval Station and Harbour of Refuge, for either or both of which purposes it offers very great facilities, and is much better adapted to them than St. Catherine's Bay, where such large and expensive works are being carried on, but which are pronounced to be a failure.

Perhaps it is now time to say a few words about the house, or hotel of the bay, for there is only one dwelling in the neighbourhood, the nearest to it being at the top of the hill more than half a mile off. It was a very good old-fashioned house situated at the bottom of the hill, facing the road leading to the pier, the side windows looking on to the sea towards Rozel.

This was a house of no pretensions to architectural beauty, and some few years ago was doubtless of a very primitive character. It was a plain white fronted house with a very deep red tiled roof, but it is useless entering into a description of it for the benefit of future visitors, as most probably before these pages meet the eye of the public, it will be metamorphosed into a handsome commodious modern building. There was a large open space in front of the house, which somewhat resembled a farm-yard, for our traveller found here a horse, a colt, a cow, dogs, geese and chickens. Perhaps my readers will want to know something of the inmates of this house. Well, then, the family consisted of mine host, hostess and several sons and daughters.

It may be expected that, as Hobbler was about to take up his abode here for some time, that I should give a full, true and particular account of these inhabitants of his Jersey home, but this I have no intention of doing. But I will say this much, that mine host was a very pleasant and intelligent companion, as was also mine hostess, and together with their daughters and sons were not only ready and willing to make their visitors comfortable and happy in their house, but were studious to do so by many of those little attentions, which soon make a man of a sociable turn of mind perfectly at his ease; and our traveller might be said to be of rather that order, that is to say he was a little convivially disposed in his temperament. And so it was not long before he was quite at home. Behold him then "the lame man of Bouley" as he was sometimes called, wandering about this bay, and killing time, as some folks say, at the sea-side. He did not call it so, for killing time can only be applied where the day hangs heavy on one's hands, which it certainly did not in his case.

Well, then, how did he amuse himself in this outlandish place, where he was once asked if he did not think he was being buried alive? Like other folks, he ate and drank, and slept when he could, which latter was not very regularly, as Morpheus and he were not on the very best of terms. He rose rather late, it must be confessed, but then that was his misfortune, not his fault, for had his health allowed him, he would have dearly loved to have risen with the lark, and drank in those delicious early morning breezes, which are not only delightful to the feelings, but are also so conducive to health; and he read a little, and talked a little (perhaps a good deal, for he was somewhat given that way at times) and he thought and observed a little, and then he mused somewhat on what he saw and heard. And various other ways he amused himself, and so time past swiftly away. One of his principal amusements was to seat himself in an arm-chair outside the front door, on a piece of green sward that ran along before the hotel, where he saw many people come and go from this lonely house by the sea-shore. And who were these people, and what did they come for? There were some of all sorts, and their errand was the pursuit of pleasure and amusement. This was one of the most favourite places in the island for pic-nics, and in the summer months, parties of this description, as well as non-pic-nic parties, were the order of the day on a wholesale scale.

Early in the day they arrived, and late in the evening they took their departure. They came on foot, in carriages, in chaises, on horseback, in omnibuses, and sometimes in boats. Some came to see and enjoy the beautiful sea and charming scenery of the bay, and some to enjoy the luxury of the bath and to gambol on the shore.

A few came there to study that peculiar art, which always requires two persons; no more no less, to work out the problem; and they must not be of the same sex. To be bold, I mean the art of love-making, for the rocky and secluded nooks of the bay are very favourable for such a course of study. But the majority came there for a far more sublunary purpose.

They came to eat and drink, and if our traveller's vision did not very much deceive him, the size of the provision baskets and hampers, in comparison with the size of the party for whose use they were intended, would often lead him to infer that a great many came there to stuff. Pic-nic parties of all descriptions came to Bouley. These parties were generally a mixture of natives and visitors; indeed, in almost all cases they are got up by the inhabitants of St. Heliers as a little treat for their friends, who may happen to be on a visit to them, though this does not follow as an invariable rule, the Jersey folks sometimes choosing to enjoy themselves by themselves.

Of the pic-nic parties, there is not a great deal to be said. They were rather exclusive during the time the feeding was going on, after this they generally rambled about the pier, or climbed the neighbouring rocks, or sat and threw stones in the water, a very favourite amusement at all watering-places. They usually took themselves off early, and did very little for the benefit of the house, and paid as little as possible for the accommodation they enjoyed. But we will leave the pic-nics and proceed to take a look at the visitors to the hotel, and the general visitors, non-pic-nics.

And Hobbler sat by the wayside in his old arm-chair, with his sticks beside him, and his newspaper in hand, over the top of which paper he peeped at holiday man and his holiday manners, as they came tripping into this pleasant sea-side abode.

And into that house he saw to enter, from day to day, a never ending variety of the genus homo.

One day there would come there the Lordly Peer, and perhaps, in contrast, the lowly beggar, though the visits of nobility are not very frequent, and happily beggars are very scarce; but still they both come at times, and both may happen to meet. At other times, would appear members of the real, the born aristocracy, side by side with those of the newly made or monied aristocracy; the one bearing their honours meekly, though conscious of their dignity, unostentatious, but not demeaning themselves—the others haughty, overbearing, and purse proud, full of display, and ever wakeful as to their position, and careful not to forego the smallest tittle of the importance that wealth always carries with it. Here in fact he saw the real gentlefolks, and the would-be gentlefolks; the one wearing their rank and position like a well-fitting garment, the other appearing as if they were dressed in borrowed robes. Here also came the well-to-do shopkeeper and members of that portion of the middling classes of society, who not being overburdened with education, and taking what is termed an outing in the summer time for the sake of enjoying themselves, give their minds up most thoroughly to the pursuit of enjoyment, and, as a rule, they generally find it in some shape or other.

A large class who visited these parts were the "clerks." Clerks from London, and clerks from all parts of the country, who snatching the small space of time allowed them for relaxation from business during the finer months of the year, rush off to these charming Isles, and place the ocean between them and the land of their hard toil, and strive, in the few short days of their residence abroad, to forget how in the sweat of their brows they earn their bread, by putting their bodies to the same test in the pursuit of pleasure. And not only does our traveller see men of all classes, all trades and all professions, but of all sizes, shapes and character. But the particular specimen of mankind, which more than any other attracted his attention, or rather obtruded itself upon his notice, was that class formerly very abundant, now fast dying out ; the true, genuine Cockney.

Now by Cockney, I do not mean so much the inhabitant of the City of London, or rather I should say I do not mean all the inhabitants of that city, but rather that particular portion of them whose ideas are shut up in that great metropolis. They live there, perhaps were born there, they rarely leave it, and when they do, either by inclination or compulsion soon hasten back to it.

Their livelihood lies there, so do nearly all their pleasures. They stand behind a counter all day, and they sport at the various places of amusement in London all the evening. They are, in fact, the fixtures, or part of them, of London. And yet they are nobody there, and they know it, and they feel that everybody else knows it. But when they go out of town, they imagine they are somebody, and vainly think that everybody will believe them to be somebody.

But everybody don't. Query does anybody? Certainly Hobbler did not think so from the sample he saw at Bouley Bay. They would come down on foot, in chaises, or even on horseback, but the majority of them came by the omnibus that professed to go round the island in one day. But, however, and whenever they came, they amused themselves invariably in the same way, for the great aim of all of them appeared to be, who could perpetrate the greatest amount of mischief in the smallest given time.

On one occasion, you might see the Militia uniform, belonging to one of the sons of mine host, appear on the backs of half a dozen men of different sizes in an almost incredible space of time, each one having his strut, and fancying himself a gallant son of Mars. At another time, four or six big men might be seen hanging on to the halyards of a flagstaff that stood in front of the house, and which was only fit to bear the weight of a boy.

Warned from there, they would snatch at the cable attached to a boat, and try to send her adrift, perfectly regardless as to whom she belonged, or as to where she went. One day our traveller being roused to a state of fiery indignation at seeing a party, a portion of which he is sorry to say belonged to the fair sex, detaching a boat from her moorings, and about to take French leave as it is called, though it is difficult to say why, Frenchmen being always so polite, and go off for a row in her; he remonstrated with them on the unfairness of such a proceeding, when he was coolly met with the enquiry as to what business he had in the matter?

Now, reader, between you and I, I don't know that he had any, but somehow or other he had so identified himself with the place, that he thought it incumbent on him to act as special constable, though most certainly not a very efficient one in case of a row.

However, to return to my tale. He replied to their rather impertinent question, that he had a great deal of business in the matter, as he did not wish to see the boat go on the rocks and be knocked to pieces, of which there really was some danger, if unskilfully handled. And what if she does, what's that to you? was again the interrogation. Hobbler now fully roused to anger, answered that in such a case they might perhaps lose their lives, which was very likely of no consequence to anybody, but the loss of the boat would be quite another affair, and if they did not desist he would find somebody to make them. This threat did not require to be put into execution, for the fact of being placed at a lower value than the boat, took all the pluck out of them, and they started off in pursuit of some fresh object, on which to exhibit their mischievous propensities. But I must let them pass, only adding, " that of course they always left their names engraven upon the windows and doors of the hotel, upon the pier, the rocks, the cliffs, and in fact upon every place within their reach, for the edification of all future comers. Before quite leaving them, I must in justice say that they decidedly added life to the scene, and that fully appearing to enjoy themselves in their own peculiar way, and only being down at the bay for a few hours during the day, our traveller is not quite satisfied that he would, if he could, have dispensed with their company altogether, for they certainly did afford him much amusement, despite his occasional exhibition of ire towards them, and they did make the place seem so delightful when they were gone. When they were gone, and when every body was gone, and before every body came. Ah! here was the great charm of the place. The hotel being of small size, there was but little accommodation for sleeping visitors, and consequently the greater part of those who came to see the bay were only there during the day, and before they arrived, and after they departed, the whole neighbourhood appeared to belong to the inmates of the hotel, as with the exception of a few stragglers, who came to enjoy their bath, and perhaps a few fishermen, they had it all to themselves. Though not a very early riser, he did on more than one occasion manage to see the beautiful orb of day rise from his watery bed; and a charming sight it was, and well repaid even an invalid for foregoing some of his, perhaps, needful rest.

Grand and glorious was the uprising of day's great luminary, as like an awaking giant, he shook himself free from night's trammels, and climbing the eastern sky, shed his benignant and life-giving influence on all surrounding nature. The sea sparkled with delight, the earth sent up its incense of thanksgiving, all nature teemed with joy and gladness, and man, Nature's great master-piece, awoke from his slumbers, went forth to his labours, and sung his morning hymn of praise to that Almighty Being, who called the Universe into existence, who said, "let there be light, and there was light," and who made the sun to rule the day, and by its glorious light and genial heat to gladden his heart, and cheer him on his weary way.

> "He looks in boundless majesty abroad,
> And sheds the shining day, that burnished plays
> On rocks, and hills, and towers, and wandering streams."

And often of a night our traveller went forth to see the sun's fair bride, as she emerged from her silvery caverns in the ocean. Rising from out its midst she illumed the hills and rocky crags, and spread their dark shadows on its placid bosom, and with her soft pale light, shed her calm influence on all the surrounding scenery. And as he sat on that lone shore's side, he watched her gentle rays as they danced on the rippling waters, and converted the blue ocean into a lake of silver. And then those countless multitudes of orbs that bespangled the mighty firmament of heaven came forth, and in reflected glitterings lit up the bosom of the deep, and sky and ocean teemed with the light of myriads of worlds, and innumerable hosts of constellations sang their vesper hymn ; and toilworn man, and all fatigued nature, as they sank to their rest, chanted their praises to Him who made the greater light to rule the day, and the lesser light to rule the night, and who made the stars also.

"Thou azure vault, where through the gloom of night,
Thick sown, we see such countless worlds of light,
Thou moon, whose car encompassing the skies,
Restores lost nature to our wond'ring eyes."—COWPER.

When the wind was in the north, or north-east, it was a glorious sight to see the ocean, as grandly and majestically it rolled into the bay of Bouley. Sometimes dashing over the pier, and at others breaking on the rock-bound shore, it would cast its foaming spray far into the air, and then receding, carry back with it masses of shingle, and for hours this assault and retreat of the waves would keep up a ceaseless roar. The rise of the tide on this coast is very great, sometimes forty feet, and our traveller saw one tide that attained the height of nearly thirty-nine feet, which just mounted to a level with the pier, over the end of which it flowed without let or hindrance. And Hobbler found many agreeable companions in this quiet retreat, for quiet it most certainly was, except during the few hours of the day before alluded to. With some he played chess, and with some he sang, though not much of a hand at those accomplishments, and with others he talked politics, of which he was rather fond; and, moreover, London newspapers found their way down somehow or other to this outlandish spot, and told him how the exterior world went on without him. And then there was also another occupation he found, and that was the pleasant one of corresponding with his friends in England; for many and kind were the letters that found him in his lonely sea-shore abode, and came in the place of their writers to ask him of his state and doings. And often of an afternoon when the postman was expected, did Hobbler sit in his roadside chair, and wait the arrival of this much respected official; and as he sat he mused, and these were his musings.

Hobbler on the Post Office.

What a charming thing is this post, and what a marvellous piece of machinery is this post; perhaps the most marvellous in all the world. The gear is always in good order, and very rarely is any part of this complicated piece of human mechanism pronounced to be out of working condition. And above all other posts, perhaps that of Her Majesty of England, Her Majesty's Mail, as it is called, is—par excellence, at any rate to an Englishman, *the* post.

Look at its workings. You have a friend hundreds of miles off. You are separated beyond the power of ordinary communication; time, perhaps, if not expense, precludes your travelling to see each other. And yet you can communicate, you can converse with your friend by means of this charming post, this faultless piece of mechanism; as faultless certainly as anything of man's invention; for where one letter miscarries, hundreds of thousands are safely and punctually delivered. And how does this machine work, and what are the results of its workings? Like a wheel within a wheel, it commences from one little centre, and then extends its ramifications over the whole universe. It maintains good fellowship between acquaintances, it cements the holy bond of brotherhood between real friends, and in fact performs very many of the social duties of man towards his neighbour.

By it the statesman and the merchant princes of the earth transact much of their business, as well as the tradesman and the private individual; and by it man supplies more or less indirectly his daily wants. The master often engages his servant by means of this post, and by this same medium the servants accept their servitude. By it parents or guardians seek the aid of tutors or governesses for their children and wards; and by it the instructors of youth seek the aid of that employment, which should, from its high character, be remunerative, but alas, is how often but the barest competence. By it the rich merchants and bankers bid for the services of their clerks, and by it the clerks accept their positions, which sometimes is one endowed with liberality, but is too frequently only a meagre subsistence. By it too the author and the composer will communicate with their publisher in the hopes of finding the reward that sweetens labour, and a profitable employment for their time and genius ; and by it they too will learn that mental labour, except of the higher order, or where it panders to some peculiar or popular taste, cannot compete in money value with mechanical labour, thus perhaps reversing in some degree the favourite theory of the power of mind over body. But pass we on. By this said post the fond mother or father holds affectionate converse with their absent child ; and who shall tell what countless messages of parental love are daily committed to its charge. And by it the child corresponds with its parent, it may be to reciprocate the affectionate outpourings of their yearning hearts, or it may be to spurn them. And also by this post the lawyer corresponds with his client, and the client with his legal adviser, and both perhaps with the unlucky object of their correspondence. And by it, though last not least, the lover corresponds with his mistress, and the mistress with her lover, and evil be to them, who would, by broken seals, or misdirected missives, avail themselves of their position, to lift the veil that hangs over their sacred correspondence. A trust is confided to the officers of her Majesty's Post Office, which they dare not betray. And it might be added, that to this extraordinary piece of machinery is confided, it were vain to tell, how many catalogues of hopes, joys, and pleasures anticipated, realised, and disappointed, also of heart-rendings, tales of woe, sorrow, appeals for mercy, &c. And the wonderful cheapness of this post places it within the reach of all classes, and before long it is to be hoped that foreign nations will more fully reciprocate the advantages offered by this country, and that some day we shall have an universal penny post. All thanks to the prime mover of this great public boon, Mr. Rowland Hill, to whom it is not saying too much, that all classes are deeply indebted.

But "letters for you Mr. Hobbler," so the postman had arrived, and our traveller's musings were suddenly cut short, and he proceeded to demonstrate the practical, rather than the theoretical machinery of the wonderful post.

In the parlour of the hotel, the visitors will be attracted by a plainly framed testimonial hanging against the walls, and such an one as many a noble family would be glad to possess, for as one of our great writers says, "brave deeds are a man's ancestors;" this is a noble heirloom to transmit to his family by the brave performer of the deed recorded thereon. Two years ago, as two very young children were bathing or playing on the rocks, some hundred yards or so from the hotel, they tumbled into the sea. Their mother, who was very near them, hastened to their rescue, but also unfortunately fell in. My worthy host, then in his sixty-fifth year, was standing at his door, and seeing these poor creatures drowning, ran down to the rocks, and without a moment's consideration as to the danger of the act, plunged into the sea after them with all his clothes on, and succeeded in rescuing all of them from a watery grave.

To comment on such an action is unnecessary. In the words of the Humane Society's testimonial, it is characterised as extraordinarily noble and gallant conduct, and no words of mine could add to his reward.

Indeed none are wanting; brave deeds always carry their own reward with them, in the delight they must always afford to the brave man in performing them.

At Bouley Bay, our traveller met with many pleasant people among the visitors who came to reside some time in the house. Of course, there were some curious and some funny ones among them, whom he is sorry he has no time to describe here; but the generality of those, whom it was his lot to meet during his residence down there, he found to be pleasant, intelligent and agreeable companions. Some of them resided in the house for several weeks, and during their stay, there sprung up between several of them and Hobbler a strong intimacy, which was maintained in many cases for some time after they had quitted Jersey, through the medium of the pleasant post. There is nothing more delightful when travelling about, than to meet with intellectual and agreeable companions, and our traveller has to acknowledge that it has almost always been his good fortune to do so. Travelling friendships are, however, unfortunately of a very fleeting character.

With several of his friends he kept up, as has been said, a correspondence, but it was only for a time. It gradually died out in a few months, and though perhaps the fault was his own, for he had several invitations to visit his new friends—still it was as he had ever found it on a journey, or when sojourning for a short time in one place, especially an hotel. You meet charming companions, you spend days of pleasant intercourse together, an apparently warm friendship springs up between you, and promises are made perhaps of sincere and enduring amity. But you part. You miss your friends very much at first, perhaps they miss you, provided you have made yourself agreeable. You probably write to them to know of their state and whereabouts, you may hear from them to make the same enquiries after yourself. You journey on, if not through fresh scenes of country, at any rate through fresh scenes of life, you meet other companions, or you return to your usual avocations; and you forget, yes it is too true, you forget, and beyond doubt you are forgotten. At first, perhaps, your recollection of your travelling companions only fades imperceptibly away, like a dissolving view on the first introduction of a new picture, as their memory of you also fades; but after a very short lapse of time, when your thoughts do by any chance recur to the pleasant days you spent together, alas! it is only but the veriest ghost of a friendship that is written down on the tablets of your memory. Yes, the events will often be affectionately cherished in sweet remembrance, when the actors in them have long passed beyond the pale of your recollection, and their names are buried in the oblivious recesses of forgetfulness. Such are travelling friendships. Such has our traveller ever found them to be; though, perhaps, on this occasion, he may have found them of a more sincere character, as the unfortunate state of his health attracted the kind-hearted towards him, more than would otherwise have been the case; and as the recorder of his thoughts and wishes, I beg leave to offer to any of those kind friends who gave their sympathies, their company, and their time to aid in lightening the suffering of our poor crippled traveller, his warmest and grateful thanks, though probably none of them will ever read these pages. Hobbler had not the most exalted ideas of the unselfishness of human nature. In his experience he had found it rather hard, but he is most willing and most delighted to acknowledge, that there is much and genuine kindness to be met with in the world, and that on the occasion of his wanderings in search of health, he met with much more than he either expected or deserved.

There is an excursion round the island every day by omnibus, very cheap, and very—but no matter what. Our traveller did not like these excursions, perhaps our readers might not either; though I certainly think they would like to get round somehow, which seems almost to be a hopeless case, while our traveller continues to moralize upon mischievous cockneys, romantic moonshines, wonderful posts, and fleeting friendships.

But we will get on. The Bouley Bay coach shall not stop up the road any longer. The fact is, that our traveller was so charmed with the beautiful scenery and sweet retirement of this spot, as well as so comfortable in his quarters there, that he did not like moving. Added to this, the fact that he was an invalid, and the weather was what, in moderately constructed phrases, is called broiling, and it is not to be wondered at. Yes, at this time people were exclaiming all day long, " well I never," or " did you ever," or in Jersey language, " oh, my good," (an expression used by all classes of society throughout the island.) I never felt anything to equal it in all my life. This expression, if they were not very chicken aged, they had probably uttered hundreds of times before.

Hobbler then came to the conclusion that Bouley Bay was not Jersey, though one of its gems, neither was it the Channel Islands, but only a very small portion of them. So he moved off, and I will now suppose him about to introduce my readers to the other beauties of Jersey, as well as those of the neighbouring islands, after his inspection of which, I have no doubt we shall meet him again if we should stroll down that pretty hill to Bouley, in which quiet retreat it is his intention to locate himself for the rest of the season.

CHAPTER III.

GENERAL VIEW OF THE ISLAND OF JERSEY.

The size of the Island and general appearance.—How to see the Island.—Description of its beautiful bays, and charming coast scenery.—Its valleys, lanes, and roads.—Its orchards, flowers and beautiful cows.— Hobbler's ruminations on the scenery of Jersey. —The romance of man's life.—The people of Jersey.—Their Dress.—Their industry and penuriousness, and general character. —Their great prosperity and its causes.—Their Laws.—Society. —Lack of English Sports.—Clameur de Haro.

THE Island of Jersey, the largest and most important of all the Channel Islands, lying, as has been said, within a bay of France, is about forty miles in circumference, taking its coast line; its greatest length at any part being about ten miles, and its greatest breadth about six.

Almost the whole of this island is richly cultivated, and it abounds in luxuriant scenery. The whole of its coast line is wild and magnificent it being literally an iron bound coast, though some of its bays are exquisitely verdant.

But, kind readers, our traveller will now, if you will allow him, take you an excursion round the island and through the island, in order that you may view the wildness of its coast scenery with all its beautiful bays, that you may travel over its admirable roads, that you may wander through its charming shady lanes, and that you may revel in its exquisite, and most justly celebrated valleys.

Now it is not my intention to divide the island into different day's excursions, as is usually done by guide books (I have already stated that I have no intention of writing a guide book); but I would rather recommend to a traveller to read a description of a place before he visits it, and with the aid of a map to chalk out for himself his day's route. If he is very much pressed for time, he should take a private vehicle of some sort, and drive through the principal parts of the country, especially in Jersey, where the hire of horses and carriages is so cheap. But I would especially advise him, that if he has plenty of time at his disposal when visiting these islands, and is a good pedestrian, by all means to walk it; for our traveller, though now physically incapacitated for doing so, was not in this case on his first visit to Jersey, some few years ago, when he enjoyed the treat of walking over the island, and is quite convinced from his experience, that though a great deal may be seen by riding, the only way really to see and appreciate all the beauties of the country, is by a tramping excursion.

I will now take the different places worth seeing, in something like the order that they occur on the map; not pledging myself, however, to any particular rule, but dotting them down in the order that they occurred to our traveller's memory when recounting his adventures; for though I am about to put these visits all in one chapter, they did not take place in any regular succession, many of them occurring after he had returned to Bouley, and we only put them together for the sake of bringing his rambling ideas into something a wee bit shapeable. I will now accordingly endeavour to give a brief description of all the principal beauties of the Island of Jersey.

Starting from St. Heliers eastward, we will proceed round the coast.

Passing along St. Clement's Bay, and Grouville Bay, the first place we arrive at of any note is Gorey. Neither the Bay of St. Clement's, or that of Grouville are particularly interesting.

The former is completely studded with rocks, stretching as far as eight or ten miles out to sea. Somewhere about the centre of this bay is a pretty little place called Pontac, where there is a very comfortable hotel. This place is much visited by the townspeople. The shores of both the above named bays are very flat. The villages of the same names as the bays are decidedly pretty, especially Grouville, which has one of the most picturesque churches in the island. These villages both lie a little inland.

On crossing Grouville Bay, the distant castle of Mount Orgueil comes into view, soaring high amongst the clouds, with the town of Gorey lying immediately beneath it. This is a very picturesque scene, especially when viewed from a distance, and doubly so when the oyster fleet is in the harbour. The old weather-beaten castle standing aloft on its rocky crag, looks down a sort of grim old giant upon the small houses and small vessels below, over which it appears to mount guard, like some huge sentinel ever watchful on his post. In former days, this castle was doubtless of great strength, but since the introduction of cannon it has become of but little use, provided an enemy could get possession of the neighbouring heights which completely command it. There is, however, some talk of fortifying these heights, and erecting large barracks there. The town of Gorey is the third and in fact the last of the Jersey towns, no other places in the island laying claim to that distinction but St. Heliers, St. Aubin, and this place.

This town is particularly interesting to the tourist on account of its fleet of oyster boats, which in the season, from the beginning of September to the end of April, are constantly, to the number of three or four hundred, going in and out of the harbour. When they are sailing in, or sailing out, or lying in port, this immense forest of masts forms a very pretty object in the landscape. There are two or three decent inns here, so that the traveller need not starve; and to those enjoying a little life, Gorey is by no means a bad place to stop at, as independant of the aforesaid fleet of oyster boats, there is always lying in the harbour, or its neighbourhood, a small steamer bearing her

Majesty's pennant, sent there for the especial protection of the oyster fishery and fishermen; these latter (principally Englishmen) being a terrible set of fellows who are always getting into hot water by fishing nearer the French coast than they are allowed by law to do, poaching as it is termed, when they are sure to be chased by a French cutter or steam vessel, and the English war vessels ought always to be there to see fair play. Many are the tales of hair breadth escapes, and wonderful stern chases that one hears from these hardy and daring seamen.

Mount Orgueil has a good deal of history attached to it. The great French general Du Guesclin, in the reign of Edward III., besieged it, but was compelled to retire from before its walls. Once the French obtained possession of it, but did not hold it long, being driven out by the islanders and the English before they held it six months. It was held successfully for sometime against the Parliamentary troops in the time of the Commonwealth, but was compelled eventually to submit to them. Originally it was a very strong fortress, but it is now fast falling to decay, though many parts are still in a good state of preservation.

Charles the Second remained in this castle for several months, and the celebrated Prynne was confined there for upwards of three years.

From the top of the keep, an extensive view can be obtained of the coast of France, and also of the neighbouring parts of the island. Leaving Gorey and climbing the hill at the back of the castle, the country that the traveller now sees before him is altogether of a different character to that he has previously viewed, and instead of the low flat shores, such as those of St. Clement's and Grouville Bays just described, he comes suddenly upon that beautiful high land, wild and rugged in some places, and richly wooded and fertile in others, for which this island on its north and north-eastern sides is so celebrated.

The first place of any note after leaving Gorey is Ann Port, as charming a little spot of earth as the eye can rest on.

This is a small bay backed by richly clad and beautifully verdant hills, descending precipitately to the shore, and on a bright summer's day with its glassy and lake-like waters, and picturesque shore, is altogether a luxuriant scene whether viewed from the lofty hills above or from a boat at sea.

The next bay is St. Catherine's, a very pretty spot, but the works of man are here predominant over those of nature, for this bay is mostly remarkable for the enormous government works carried on here, in the shape of piers, &c., to form a harbour of refuge and a naval station. These works, however, it is thought will be abandoned, although nearly completed, as it is said there is not a sufficient depth of water for large vessels. If this be the case, it must be confessed to be a most terrible waste of public money, upwards of half a million of English money has already been spent upon these works, and one cannot help thinking that there must have been frightful jobbery somewhere. But our business is not with such matters just now, but rather to revel in the beauties of nature which, in this part of the island, come upon us thick and threefold, for at every turn you take, new ones burst upon the view in almost endless variety. The works at St. Catherine's are well worthy of inspection, and the roads leading down to this bay and to Ann Port are both of them wild, precipitous, and picturesque.

After passing the north-eastern point of the island known as La Coupe, in the neighbourhood of which are some very interesting Druidical remains, the roads descends a very steep hill which leads to the village and harbour of Rozel.

Rozel is a sweet little bay, or creek, with a small but rather pretty village, consisting of a few old fashioned houses scattered about here and there, the whole overhung by cliffs and hills of a very bold character, which in many places are crowned with luxuriant foliage, and in others present a wild and sterile appearance. On one of these hills are some beautifully laid out gardens belonging to a Mr. Curtis, which he generously allows the public to view. Here he has succeeded in growing on an almost barren rock all sorts of eastern and rare plants.

There is a small harbour here, but it is only capable of admitting small craft. A most charming and secluded lane runs up from this bay into the interior of the island. Rozel is well worthy of a visit, and whether viewed from the surrounding hills or from the shore is very pretty. There is a comfortable hotel here, where the traveller can refresh his wearied body, after having mentally feasted upon the rich draughts of bounteous nature around him.

Leaving Rozel and travelling onwards towards

Trinity, we pass through a valley so richly wooded and so exceedingly beautiful altogether, that it is difficult to say whether it is surpassed by any in the island. The road gradually winds up the side of the hill, leaving the valley which runs on a level at the bottom further and further below you as you ascend, until when you reach the top of the hill, you find it some hundred feet perpendicularly beneath your feet. The valley down in the bottom is very narrow, the opposite hill rising very abruptly within a short distance of the base of the one in which the road is cut. This opposite hill is most richly clad with foliage, and the valley at your feet most exquisitely green and suggestive of all that is cool and refreshing, a sweet little murmuring stream, full of water-cresses, running through its entire length.

The country, or rather the coast from Rozel to Bouley, is of a very wild character, but the ride along the road is a charming one, and perhaps there is nothing more beautiful than the view from this part of the island on a calm autumnal evening at sunset. Looking westward, far below you is the little pier of Bouley, with the beautifully clear waters of its bay, the bold rocks stretching away in the distance and glowing in the refulgent light of departing day. The glorious ocean lies beyond, with the Islands of Serk and Guernsey reposing on its placid bosom, and far away to the northward, Cape La Hogue on the coast of France, and the Island of Alderney in the extreme distance, all more or less illumined by the beautifully subdued, but nevertheless brilliant, tints of the setting sun. Many a time has our traveller lingered on these heath-covered hills to gaze upon the beauty of this landscape, as viewed under the influence of the fading day.

Passing onward we come to Bouley, which has already been fully noticed.

The next bay to Bouley is Bonne Nuit, another charming spot; but there are so many of these charming spots, that all that can be said to the tourist is, go and see them, and judge for yourself.

Bonne Nuit is particularly charming to the lover of wild and grand scenery, and forms, like Bouley, a beautiful contrast to some of the richly wooded nooks that we have already passed.

Passing on again round the coast, we come to one of the pets of the tourist, Grève de Lecq.

Your approach to this bay is through a valley of

a somewhat similar character to the one described as leading from Rozel, though of a much greater length. It is a very narrow valley, running between two lofty, precipitous and richly clothed hills. It is beautifully verdant, and at some parts very grand. The road which winds along the side of one of the hills gradually descends to the shore, after running a long distance through this narrow valley, or it might almost be termed pass, only that passes are perhaps generally understood to be roads through rocky mountains, and not through luxuriantly verdured hills.

But at last you reach the bottom, when the full view of the sea bursts suddenly upon you, quite unlike Bouley, where the whole prospect is stretched out before you immediately you commence the descent. Arrived at the shore, you find the hotel standing almost on the sands. This is the hotel where the excursion omnibus takes all its passengers to dine at. At least it did so in 1858. Now there is an opposition, or perhaps several. But a word or two about these excursions "all round the Island in one day." To be bold, our traveller considered them to be all a myth, for far from being any great boon it is quite the reverse, and in making this remark he would not wish for one moment to influence the public to the detriment of any of the parties connected with these excursions, neither does he think his observations have any tendency to do so.

Now, most people coming alone to Jersey, and having only a short time to stop there, generally go to an hotel, in which case they are always sure to find plenty of folks ready and willing to join them in the expense of a carriage for the day. The cost of a carriage with a pair of horses, one that will hold six people, is fourteen shillings; or a four wheeled chaise to hold four persons is eight shillings. In either case, the whole expense, including coachman (if you require one) and baiting, most certainly would not exceed three shillings a head. The fare by the omnibus is two shillings. One shilling a piece in a day's amusement is certainly not very much, when people go so far as Jersey in search of it. By the omnibus, you are led to believe you see all the beauties of the island, but you do nothing of the sort; but on the contrary miss many of the gems, and pass through many very uninteresting parts, whereas by your own conveyance, you can see nearly all the beauties, and skip those places that are not worth seeing, to say nothing of the advantage of being able to stop when and where you like, and to remain out all day if you wish it.

But to return to Grève de Lecq. It really is a very beautiful place, though in the estimation of our traveller somewhat overrated. The cliffs rise here to a great height perpendicularly, and the scene is altogether one of a very wild character. Inglis says that Grève de Lecq is approached through a narrow and deep valley of a wild but beautiful aspect, bounded by nearly perpendicular cliffs, and offering alike in its form and situation, and general features a perfect picture of a solitary island cove. Grève de Lecq has this advantage over Bouley, that the beach is composed of soft sand, whereas at the latter place it is all shingle. This is also a famous place for pic-nics; parties of this description may be seen here on a bright summer's day by the dozen. In the neighbourhood, are some celebrated caves at a point called Plemont. Our traveller inspected these on one of his previous visits to Jersey; but their being rather difficult of access, and when reached requiring a steady head and firm limbs to go through them, of course he did not venture there on this occasion. He would, however, remark that their inspection will amply reward the traveller for his fatigue and trouble. They are not approachable at all times of the tide, therefore the stranger should procure a guide before making the attempt.

We now approach the north-western point of the island, on which stands the ruins of an old castle, known as Grosnez Castle, the point being Grosnez Point. This castle, or rather its ruins, is supposed to be one of the things that were in the days that the mighty Roman ruled the world, as some of the guide books carry the date of its building as far back as the times of those mighty conquerors.

In coming to Jersey, somebody on board the packet is almost sure to point out to you the resemblance which this headland bears to the head of Louis Phillipe. One of the guide books says it is like the head of Napoleon, but our traveller says he traced something like an image of the former, but though looking for it on several occasions, he could not discover any resemblance to the great conqueror of Europe. And now we come to the western side of Jersey, the greater part of which, as far as the coast line is concerned, is comprised in St. Ouens' bay, the most barren, the most extensive, and perhaps the most uninteresting of all the bays, though its very wild and dreary character carries with it a great charm; and Hobbler is far from certain that had he been living nearer to St. Ouens than he was, but what he should have paid it many visits, and perhaps revelled in the rugged and desolate scenery of its bay, for when a man's walk through life has been rather of a rugged character, there is somewhat in this kind of scenery that fuses with his ideas, assimilates with his disposition, and charms his mind when the melancholy mood is upon him.

But let us pass on, and view a scene of a different character. Passing round by La Corbière, the south-western point of the island, and the wildest perhaps of all its wild spots, we come to St. Brelades' bay, which take it for all in all, is, perhaps, par excellence the favourite with the majority of the visitors. And not unjustly so either. Not so extensively beautiful as St. Aubins or St. Ouens, or so wild as Grève de Lecq, or so grand as Bouley, it may be said to be a combination of them all to a certain extent, and is altogether a most lovely and most imposing spot.

The bay is divided into two parts by an enormous mass of rocks, which stand out from the shore; but the part which principally attracts the visitor is the western end, where is to be seen the old church, which though a building of no great pretensions to architectural beauty, from its general character and situation harmonises so charmingly with all around it, that the eye is fain to wander again and again to its venerable and antiquated walls. Covered with ivy of many varieties, and partly embosomed in trees, standing on the edge of a rock or cliff, the sea lapping up to the very foot of its time-honored walls, it forms a sweet foreground to this picture of the bay, which is shut in on the land side by a beautiful curve of hills richly clad with luxurious vegetation, a sequestered villa occasionally peeping out from behind the dense foliage, or a charming little homestead with the beautiful Alderney cow wandering about its paddocks, crowning the brow of the hill. The shores of this bay are composed of soft white sand, almost as smooth as velvet.

Altogether it presents such an exquisite picture of quiet repose, as exemplified in beautiful scenery, that not only does the traveller linger there and find difficulty in tearing himself away from it, but it is one of those sweet scenes that memory will often recall and paint anew on the mind's eye, and which leaves its impress so deeply engraven on memory's tablets that they are rarely, if ever, effaced. And St. Brelades is not wanting either in the wild or the grand. Passing round a point by the church, one is most struck by the contrast presented to the scenery we have just surveyed. Wild and rugged rocks, without a particle of vegetation, are there piled one on the other, against which Neptune and Boreas hurl their furious assaults with but little if any effect. Loud roars the blast, and madly dashes on the angry billows, but they dash and roar in vain ; those time-riven rocks and tempest-beaten shores are proof against all assaults. "Hitherto shalt thou come, but no further, and here shall thy proud waves be stayed," is the fiat that has gone forth from that Almighty Power, who holds the wind and waves in the hollow of His hands, and against it the elements fall powerless.

The roads from St. Brelades to St. Aubins wind over a very steep hill, and are of a very rugged character, but the one furthest inland goes through a beautiful valley, and is a very picturesque ride.

This road is not the one usually frequented; but both roads lead into St. Aubins town.

There is a small bay or cove between St. Brelades' bay and the bay of St. Aubins, called Portelet; the easternmost end of which is Noirmont Point, which latter forms the western boundary of St. Aubins' bay. Portelet bay was formerly the quarantine ground, and there is a sad tale told here of a whole ship's crew dying of the plague, their captain falling the last victim. There is a large rock here known as Janvrin's tomb, named after this poor captain.

Of the town of St. Aubins, our traveller has not much to say. In the days of yore it was the capital of Jersey, but it has long since been supplanted by its powerful rival St. Heliers. The bay of St. Aubins has been fully described in the first chapter of this book.

Having now passed round the coast, let us take a glance at the interior of the island, though I have already attempted in one or two places to give an idea of some of its valleys. The valley of Rozel, and that leading to Grève de Lecq have been described; but, perhaps, the finest of all the valleys are those leading out of St. Aubins' bay.

Here are the valleys of St. Laurence, Beaumont, and St. Peter's, all very beautiful; the latter, however, being generally considered to be most so of any in the island.

This valley starting from about the middle of the bay, runs north-west to St. Peter's village near the western coast of the island. This is truly a lovely spot, and perhaps the best drive in the island. A magnificent road, equal to almost any in England; runs on a level throughout its whole length. The hills rise on either side of you, most richly clad with bright green turf and beautiful foliage. A stream flows at your feet in many places, and here and there a water mill of quaint construction peeps out from among the trees, and adds greatly to the picturesque effect of the scene.

There is also a beautiful valley close to St. Heliers on the Trinity road, called the Val de Vaux, a favourite resort of the townspeople, but one suited only for pedestrians, as the road is not particularly good.

Another spot in the same ne'ghbourhood, called Water Lane, is quite a gem, and a most delightful walk in the cool of a summer's evening. But it is impossible to notice all the valleys in the island.

Our traveller's wish has been to describe the most prominent features of Jersey, and if he has omitted any of the bays, as well as the valleys, he has no doubt that the same description of scenery will be found in them as in some of those he has enumerated. He believes he travelled pretty well all over the island, but to attempt a description of all the places worth seeing in it, in a book of these dimensions, would be quite out of the question.

The lanes of Jersey are perhaps one of its most remarkable and beautiful features. Here you may ramble all day sheltered from the burning sun, shut in by lofty banks, in many places covered with beautiful ivys of many varieties, with a canopy of green leaves overhead through which the sun never penetrates. Of these lanes there are some hundreds of miles in the island, and the visitor who only knows the coast of Jersey, however beautiful that may be, is acquainted with but a small portion of its charming scenery. Perhaps the best time to wander in these secluded lanes is on a summer eve, when twilight is fading, and night begins to throw her dusky mantle over the skies, when the feathered tribes of heaven have gone to their roost, and when the glow-worm, which abounds in this island, sheds its light in every direction among the hedges and banks. As the poet of "The Seasons" beautifully describes it,

> " Among the crooked lanes, on every hedge,
> The glow-worm lights his gem,
> And thro' the dark, a moving radiance trembles."

The roads of Jersey are another remarkable feature. The visitor will be struck by the excellent roads which run in all directions across the island, and he will be particularly struck by the absence of turnpikes on these roads, such a thing not being known in these parts; a fact rather pleasant to the wayfarer than otherwise. These roads were constructed as military roads, and as far as general traffic is concerned, have completely superseded the old roads and lanes, but whether in case of war they would be beneficial to the island is very doubtful. Bodies of troops could doubtless be easily transported from one part of the island to another to defend any particular point of the coast that was menaced, but presuming an enemy to have effected a landing, these roads would be just as useful to them as to the Jerseymen; and they could move their army about from one place to another with increased facility. Formerly, an enemy landing in Jersey could never penetrate into the interior without prodigious loss, as not only were the ways so intricate, but every lane and every hedge was a fortress, from which, when beaten, the islanders only retired to another not fifty yards off, or perhaps even reappeared on the rear of the invading forces. In fact it was this kind of warfare in the province of La Vendée, which cost Republican France more time and men than many of her most brilliant campaigns, though here she had little else than an army of peasants to oppose her, in the place of the veteran legions of the great European empires.

Of the villages of Jersey there is not a great deal to be said. Suffice it, that the island is divided into twelve parishes, each one possessing its church and a cluster of houses, and in almost all instances two hotels or taverns, which in nearly every case are closely adjoining the church. Indeed, a good deal of parish business is carried on in these said taverns on Sunday morning after service, and sales by auction were often effected on the same day in the church-yard, but this latter practice has been stopped of late years. The most important of these villages, are St.

Saviour's, St. Martin's and St. John's, though probably there is no great pre-eminence in these over the other villages of the island. None of them are very extensive, though all are to a certain extent picturesque; for there generally being plenty of foliage in the neighbourhood, there is always to be seen "the village church among the trees, which points with taper spire to heaven," and which adds such a charm to many of the hamlets of Old England. There is a high tower in the centre of the island, called La Hogue Bie, better known as Prince's Tower. This is situated on the summit of a mount surrounded by lofty trees, the tower peeping out at the top. It is well worth the trouble of an ascent, the whole of the island lying stretched out at your feet; for as you stand on the battlement or roof, you can trace the sea for nearly the whole circle of the island.

This place, like almost all the old buildings, and all the bays, castles and prominent rocks, has its legend attached to it; but as these legends are so numerous I have not indulged in any of them, fearful that I should get involved in a labyrinth, from which I should never be able to extricate myself. But if my readers are anxious to go into this subject, and what poetic mind will not plead guilty to a little fancy that way, I refer them to the guide books, especially that by Mr. Octavius Rook, where they will find them wholesale to their heart's content.

The island of Jersey, though partly devoted to the growth of corn, may be described in a general view of it, as one large and beautiful garden, with its orchards and meadows attached.

Only a small breadth of land, comparatively speaking, is set apart for the growth of grain, for wherever you travel, you generally find a great portion of the country devoted to the cultivation, of what is commonly called garden produce, or else large meadows thickly planted with fruit trees.

The orchards present a very beautiful appearance in the spring time, especially the apple-trees. In many places you pass along lanes and narrow roads where, the trees overhanging, you have a beautiful canopy of blossoms over your head, when the blossom fades you can fancy yourself in a luxurious bower, and as the summer wears on, the green leaf, richly sprinkled with the rosy fruit hanging in graceful pendants above you, forms a most elegant and refreshing arcade.

Flowers grow in this island most luxuriantly, and with little apparent trouble bestowed upon them. The hydrangea, the fuschia and the oleander are most prolific, and attain a great state of perfection. The hydrangea, especially, may be considered as one of the marked features of the Jersey garden, generally growing to a great size and blowing two colours, purple and pink. The magnolia also grows very freely here, as well as the myrtle and the verbena, and in fact most of the flowers we find in England are to be found here of a superior kind; and many which in the mother-country require a green-house, are here grown in the open air. There is a very peculiar kind of cabbage grown in these parts, known as the Cæsarean or cow-cabbage. It is used principally for the food of cattle, though one part of it is very good for the eating of human beings. It attains a most extraordinary height, sometimes as much as ten or twelve feet. The stems are made into walking sticks, though somewhat feeble reeds to rely upon. This cabbage will not grow to any perfection in England. In speaking of the produce of the Jersey garden, we must not omit to mention the celebrated Chaumontel pear, which grows here, not only abundantly, but to such a pitch of perfection, that even its wholesale price in the market is rarely below five guineas the hundred pears. Of course this price only applies to the largest sort, the smaller ones being sold at much lower prices.

One of the most attractive objects in the country is the beautiful and elegant Alderney cow, which is bred principally in Jersey and Guernsey. The exquisitely shaped head, and finely developed form of this animal is not only the admiration of the naturalist and the painter, but is one of the greatest ornaments in the justly celebrated landscape scenery of these islands.

The farm houses, several old fashioned Manor houses, and a number of picturesque wells, are all very attractive features in the landscape, especially the latter, many of which are of a very antique character, and form a beautiful subject in the hands of an experienced artist. The villas and cottages in the country do not require any notice, being of rather an ordinary character.

As regards the cultivation of the soil in these islands, it can hardly be expected that in a small book like this the subject should be gone into. I may, however, just mention that there is a system of deep ploughing carried on here, which is very successful, for the soil being a great depth and very rich, they are, by this system, enabled periodically to bring to the surface a maiden soil, and also by constantly varying the crops, they never impoverish the land, as it is too much the custom to do in England. Add to this, the far more congenial nature of the climate, the facilities of procuring manure in the shape of vraic or sea-weed, and the hard working and industrious character of the people, and it is not to be wondered at that the produce of the Jersey farm and the Jersey garden is very much more remunerative than that of the mother country.

I have now recorded somewhat hastily Hobbler's views of the principal external features of Jersey, which, when having concluded, he was inclined to follow up with one of his everlasting musings. Fearing, however, that our book was getting very unwieldy, and that our readers would be considerably tired of his ruminations, I begged him to be very brief about them, and to condense them into as small a space as possible; whereupon he assured me that he was only thinking, how, on a review of all the pictures he had seen in this island, what a very strong resemblance some of them bore to many of the stages in man's life.

He said that in the beautiful placidity and serenity of the view in St. Brelades' bay, as well as in the peaceful valleys of the island and its luxuriant displays of floriculture, he could not help tracing a similitude to that happy time of life, when beneath the bright sunshine of a fond mother or father's love, one basks in the delightful warmth of pure happiness; when all is calm and peaceful and we float on the full tide of innocence; when the mind is at ease, and the brows untraced by care; when childish and youthful we revel in the very heyday of pure enjoyment; and when everything we view appears in gorgeous colours and richly fragrant, even as the peace of these valleys and purity of these landscapes, or the brilliant and sweet flowers of this island strike home to our senses in the bright sunlight of a summer'sday.

Again in the grandeur and wildness of Bouley bay, Bonne Nuit, and other places of a like description, he would fain fancy that he saw the landscape counterpart to that time of human life when the bud of youth is expanding into the open blossom of maturer age; when the boy becomes a man and his riper ideas begin to develope themselves; when the limited world that he has hitherto lived in begins to enlarge; when the grandness of his future life and his castle buildings tower high in prospective before him, even as these aspiring hills; and visions float before his mind's eye, of future greatness as wild and as bold as the tottering crags of these magnificent bays, though perhaps only like them destined, alas, how soon to fall and be dashed to atoms.

Again in the rugged and the desolate character of St. Ouens, and the cheerless rocks that surround this coast in all directions, without one particle of vegetation to relieve their barrenness, he imagined that he saw but too often the portraiture of that time of human existence, from which it is to be hoped that very many are exempt; when man's path through life becomes rugged and cheerless as these barren rocks, his prospects perhaps destroyed by some afflictions of Providence, and his hopes all blighted and desolated by the rude winds of adversity, even as these wild rocks are desolated and steriled by the wear of time and the terrific blasts of the elements.

And once more he would return to the sweet repose of St. Brelades, fancying that he saw painted there the peaceful enjoyment of declining life, but we must not allow our traveller to indulge in this style of reflection. Besides he cannot know aught about declining years, whatever he may do of the previous scenes, so I will abruptly terminate his musings on the romance of man's life as delineated in landscape scenery, leaving him, if very anxious to do so, to perpetuate his ideas in this metaphorical style, in the shape of moral and sentimental essays somewhere else.

To proceed, I will now endeavour to give our traveller's ideas, his descriptions and his opinions on the internal or domestic affairs of the island; and I will also endeavour to condense them as much as possible, merely just taking a glance at its inhabitants, their manners and customs, their peculiarities and their great prosperity, and perhaps a word or two about their laws.

In travelling about Jersey, one cannot fail to be struck by the general appearance of the prosperity of the islanders, and the consequent absence of poverty and beggary.

Beggars are rarely to be seen, and though the

dress of the peasantry and that of many who rank much above that class is not of a very fine texture, it is not the want of the means, but rather the want of inclination to spend money that causes them to dress so shabbily. The dress of the Jersey people may as well be noticed here. The lower classes, as a rule, dress very plainly and at a very small expense, and the richer classes in the country, at least the males, are not fond of spending much in attiring their persons; though they do try to make something of a show on Sundays, but somehow or other, it is difficult to say why, their clothes generally look as if they were cut out with a pick-axe, and put on with a pitch-fork. They seem to fancy too that it is unbusiness like to be well dressed in the week days, except Saturday, when many of them don their best in order to go to market. In the town of St. Heliers, the men of all classes dress plainly in the week, the lower classes especially so, but on Sundays they all come out smart.

As regards the dress of the female portion of the inhabitants, it is only necessary to say that quite the lower classes are plainly and cheaply clothed, whilst all the rest, throughout the island, are most extensively attired, and the remarks applied to the lady visitors in the first chapter of this book will apply with equal force to them. All young ladies officiating in shops, also wear very fashionable habiliments, as also do the servant girls, which latter are a very independant class in the island, as they appear to be in England also now a days.

Cheapness, not only in dress, but in every thing else, is the grand desideratum. In fact, the greatest characteristic of the people of this island is frugality carried to its extreme limit, and designated by many writers as penuriousness; and our traveller is compelled to state that from all he saw, while resident in Jersey, that money, or rather the getting of money, is the principal thought that occupies, from blushing morn to dewy eve, the whole mind of the population.

They rarely rest except to take their meals, and then only allow the bare time to swallow them; and altogether they may be said to be the very patterns of industry, (especially the women of the lower classes who work like slaves) though some think this never ceasing craving after money, a fact almost to be lamented as much as idleness.

In their business dealings, they drive bargains very close, but then perhaps they are contented with small profits. In the country they live on very common food always sending the best produce of their land to market. A Jerseyman is rarely if ever convicted of theft, and they are therefore considered patterns of honesty as well as industry, though some folks have been found ill-natured enough to raise a doubt as to whether such very close shaving in business is quite compatible with the pure spirit of honesty.

Jersey labour (at least agricultural labour) is not generally to be hired, for there is a kind of give and take system among the natives by which they assist one another when aid is required, and which though apparently not a very independent system, is said to work very well amongst themselves. Hired labour, if wanted, is to be found among the English, French or Irish portions of the population.

The language spoken in Jersey is now generally English, though the working classes talk a kind of patois, called Norman French, which is a terrible jargon, and quite unintelligible to either English or Frenchmen. The upper classes speak both English and French as well as the Jersey patois.

Party spirit runs very high in this island, and it matters little what improvements are suggested, without they emanate from that party in the ascendant, as there is not a shadow of a chance of their success unless proposed by the dominant power.

Education is to be had here of a very good character, and at a very moderate cost, and that at Victoria College offers many advantages for the upper, and middling classes; and many English families send their children over to Jersey and Guernsey, for the sake of receiving a cheap and good education.

The inhabitants of this island are not very celebrated for their beauty. This remark applies especially to the working classes, and the cause is most obvious. Incessant labour, combined with poor living, tells very much against the proper and handsome developement of the human frame; added to which, the general system of intermarriage which is carried out in most families, and it is not to be wondered at that the people are pronounced to be deficient both in stature and beauty. Owing to this system of intermarriage, a great portion of the population are constantly in mourning; and as a rule, many of the females in the country always wear black bonnets to be ready to meet the oft recurring season of wearing black, mourning it can scarcely be called when it is donned so constantly, for though the "inky cloak" may be accompanied by "the dejected 'haviour of the visage," it is much to be feared that they are very often but trappings and outward show.

The people of Jersey are rather of a lively turn of mind, partaking to a certain degree of the vivacity of their near neighbours the French, and are generally good-natured, civil and polite, though one somewhat misses in the country that polite and pleasant recognition from the peasantry, with which one is greeted in travelling through most parts of England, and which our traveller met with to a great extent even in the neighbouring island of Guernsey.

The religion of Jersey is principally Protestant, the Roman Catholics not mustering very strong. The Church of England numbers a large portion of the population among her members, though there are a very large proportion of dissenters of different persuasions. Party spirit runs as high in religious affairs as it does in political ones.

The Channel Islands are in the diocese of Winchester, and are visited by the Bishop every three years for the purposes of confirmation, &c. &c.

Living in Jersey is decidedly cheap, though not nearly so much as it was a few years ago.

House rent is much about the same as in England, and the principal necessaries of life are but little different in price. Land is very dear, being about £3 the vergee, or nearly equal to £7 the acre annual rent, whereas in England you can procure very first rate land at from £3 to £4 the acre.

But there is almost a complete absence of taxes, and rates are a mere nothing. The tax-gatherer is an unknown personage in these islands, and luxuries are very cheap, owing to the fact of Jersey and indeed all the group of islands being free ports, and consequently there are no custom dues to be paid.

The population of Jersey is somewhat about 64,000, the town of St. Heliers claiming nearly half the number.

The climate of this island is generally considered superior to that of England. Snow falls but very seldom, but rain in great abundance at certain seasons. On the whole it is considered a healthy place, but is somewhat notorious for the developement of rheumatic and liver complaints, and at times of excessive rain is subject to severe incursions of fever.

In summer time it is a delightful dwelling place, though the town of St. Heliers is perhaps a little too hot.

The laws of Jersey are very curious, never having been much changed since the days of King John. Some of them are perfectly unworthy of the present age, but as a Commission has been appointed by the House of Commons to enquire into them in order to rectify their abuses, it is needless to enter much into the subject. At the same time, I would advise the visitor to these parts who may have an hour to spare, to read them, and probably he might derive some amusement from their perusal; but it is imperative upon every Englishman before going to take up his residence there to make himself thoroughly acquainted with them, and when perfectly conversant on the subject to be very careful not to infringe them, especially the law of debtor and creditor, which is a very curious one.

The population of Jersey is decidedly military, every man being compelled to serve in the militia between the ages of seventeen and seventy. After residing in Jersey for more than a twelvemonth, every male between those ages is expected to take a part in the defence of the country, and for that purpose must be enrolled as a militiaman.

The Jersey people are not particularly partial to the English, though doubtless they prefer them to the French as masters, being no doubt well satisfied that if they fell under the dominion of the latter power, they would be governed by the same laws, and subjected to the same amount of taxation as any other department of France, and most certainly not retain possession of those exclusive privileges that they enjoy under the mild rule of Great Britain. In their manners they are decidedly more French than English, though the towns have not the least the appearance of French ones.

As to Jersey being able to maintain itself as an independent power, the idea is absurd; for beyond all doubt, if England withdrew her protection from the Channel Islands, they would most assuredly fall into the hands of the French.

And now let us just glance at the prosperity of

these islands. Whence comes it that the inhabitants of all these islands, and especially those of Jersey, are what is commonly called so well to do in the world?

It is doubtless owing partly to their great industry and frugality, though the great secret of it really lies in the fact that the English government has conferred commercial privileges upon these islands, which it grants to no other province of her dominions.

As has already been stated, there are very few customs duties to be paid here, and no taxes; and the Jersey people are thus placed in a position completely beyond that of the English.

French and indeed all foreign produce is imported into the island duty free. Jersey produce is imported into England duty free also. Jersey vessels are rigged with foreign cordage, which pays no duty, and her vessels were formerly constructed with untaxed timber, which latter paid a heavy duty in England.

Put these facts together—Jersey sends her own produce to England, which owing to the fertility of her soil, the mildness of her climate, the immunity which her people enjoy from rates and taxes, and the industry of her population, she can afford to send into the English market at a lower price than the growers in that country. She then imports for her own consumption, foreign produce duty free.

Take potatoes, for instance, which she can grow at a lower price than the English farmer can do. So she sends them all to the high priced market in England for sale, and goes herself to purchase in the cheap ones of France.

But I must leave these matters. I should have much liked to have gone more into the detail of the manners and customs of the people of the Channel Islands, as well as into their commercial history, but I fear I have already spun this chapter out to a most unwarrantable length, by going into topics somewhat irrelevant to the nature of my book, and will therefore bring it to a conclusion.

For a more detailed account of the people, their manners, and customs, and commercial greatness, I would refer my readers to a very admirable work written by Mr. H. D. Inglis more than twenty years ago, called the Channel Islands, which though now imperfect in some of its information, is nevertheless on the whole a correct and valuable work. Some of the information in this chapter has been gained from that work, and the author would gratefully acknowledge it, though he makes bold to say that the bulk of it has been gleaned by the personal observation of Mr. Thomas Hobbler, and that therefore that gentleman and the author are answerable for all the errors (and the latter fears they are many) contained herein.*

Let us now proceed to the conclusion of the chapter. There are numbers of English residents in the island, to whom, if the visitor gets an introduction he will find himself much in the same society as if he was in England. The behaviour of these residents is much like that of those of the mother country, though they sorely lack the sports of that sporting land.

It has already been stated that there are very few amusements in Jersey either in doors or out. There being no game in the Channel Islands, there is no shooting; there being no streams and very few ponds, there is but little fishing; and the country being of too dangerous a character, there cannot be any hunting.

---

* A digest of the laws and a great deal of statistical information may be obtained from the Independent Almanac, a very useful publication, and produced at the low price of 1s.

Having touched on the laws of Jersey, it will not be thought out of place in this chapter to notice the enforcement of one of them—a law of a most singular character, called Clameur de Haro, which took place during our traveller's residence in Jersey. I cannot do better than give the words of Inglis on this peculiar law, which is most undoubtedly a remnant of the dark ages.

"All encroachments on property, and all civil injuries which require a prompt remedy, may be resisted by the Clameur de Haro, after which an action is brought. This singular exclamation, the form of which is 'Haro, Haro, Haro, à l'aide mon Prince,' was only made use of in the Duchy of Normandy, as it existed on its first constitution, on occasions of great peril or consequence, and was an appeal made to Rollo for justice and protection, as the founder of the laws, and preserver of the rights of the people. The word Haro is compounded of Ha! an earnest ejaculation, and of a contraction of the name of the duke. But much as it was formerly respected in Normandy, it is to this day no less absolute here; it is an instantaneous check which cannot be disputed, and one of the parties must be fined!" The occasion, to which I have alluded when this law was put in force, arose from of a dispute between the rector of one of the country parishes and a portion of his congregation. It appears that he had been empowered by the Bishop of the diocese to effect certain repairs in his church. Whether he exceeded his powers our traveller does not pretend to say, but most certainly some of his proceedings were so rapid that one was almost tempted to fancy that the fairies, (which according to the legends have had a great hand in many ecclesiastical matters in this island) had been lending a helping hand; for they said that one night the parishioners had seen an old gallery in the church it its proper place, and the next day it had vanished and a pretty gothic window appeared in its stead. But to the law. It was to stop this terrible and almost supernatural improvement of the church, that one of the ill-used parishioners resorted to the terrors of this law, and launched the thunders of old Rollo upon the inno- cent workmen engaged in the repairs of the church. Down on their knees go these officers of justice, and invoking the presence doubtless of the grim old Norman, they shout out his name with the Ha! be- fore it, and woe betide the desperate man who dares resist the challenge. In this case, the men were deaf.

The old proverb says "none so deaf as those that wont hear." So thought the court, for they fined these men for disobedience of the laws, for sad to say they went on working in spite of the proclamation of this terrible Clameur de Haro.

Jersey presents many features of interest for the study of the botanist, and the geologist. The ferns of Jersey are seventeen in number, and probably others exist which have escaped the observation of the student. But I linger too long in this Island of Jersey, and the only apology I can offer my readers for doing so, is that our traveller spent the greater part of his time there. Perhaps it might be as well to add that this island is the principal one of the group, no other, excepting Guernsey, holding any comparison to it; and this latter is decidedly inferior to it in size, in population, and in the beauty of its scenery. Moreover, many of the remarks made, and descriptions given in this chapter, are intended to apply to the whole group of the Channel Islands.

We will now go to these other islands. The weather is charming, the beautiful sea most tempting, and the steamers very inviting, all ready to convey our traveller to these not very distant shores. And he, with our aid, is both ready and willing to have the honour of conveying our readers there, and to introduce them to the Lions of the neighbourhood; and I sincerely trust, between us, we shall be able to enliven the excursion with some little incident, and make it as pleasant and agreeable to our readers as possible.

"Let go the head rope. You for Guernsey, Sir? Look sharp if you please. Move her a head. Go on."

CHAPTER IV.

GUERNSEY.

St. Peter's Port.—The Landing, and shouting porters.—Castle Cornet.—Harbours.—The Fish-market.—Churches.—Dearth of Public Buildings.—General View of the Island.—Cobo Bay and "poor Billy."—Splendid scenery on the south-west coast.—Inhabitants of Guernsey.—Their Courtesy.—Their Gardens and Flowers.—Guernsey Society.

"The early birds catch the worms." So goes the old saying, and the early man catches the pure breezes of blushing morn, which inspirit his mind and invigorate his body. Now as I have before explained it, Hobbler, though he had the will to indulge in this luxury, had not always the ability to do so, but sometimes he did manage it.

On a beautiful morning in the month of August he rose from his couch almost with the lark; for after completing his toilet, and having ridden more than a mile, he found himself on board the steam-packet Express lying in St. Heliers, harbour, soon after the clock had marked the half circuit of its hour hand.

'Twas, as I have said, a glorious morning, and all nature seemed full of life and vigour, the hills rejoiced in the bright sunshine, and the sea shone like glass. The steam was up, and at half past six the vessel quitted her moorings, and lightly gliding out of port, was soon ploughing her way through the waters of the ocean, leaving her foamy track behind her glittering in the sunbeams, which danced upon the frothy waves, sometimes in pure white crystals, and at others in all the prismatic colours of the rainbow.

Before nine o'clock, the shores of Guernsey were reached, and soon after that hour our traveller found himself seated in a comfortable hotel in the Town of St. Pierre la Porte, partaking of an excellent breakfast for which his unwontedly early journey had given him more than his wonted appetite.

On approaching Guernsey from Jersey, one gets a peep at the prettiest part of the coast, having a distant view of one or two of its most beautiful bays.

Unlike the island last named, Guernsey's beauties

lie on the south, and south-west of it; the northern and eastern parts, present a very wild, flat and uninteresting appearance. Before entering the port, we pass a large Castle, built on a rock some distance from the shore, which somewhat reminds one of Elizabeth Castle at St. Heliers. This is called Castle Cornet.

On landing at St. Peters, one encounters something of the same kind of nuisance in the way of contending porters as at St. Heliers, though here they are certainly under some degree of control, as no man can come to take your baggage unless called by number. How you are to choose, it is somewhat difficult to determine, when all are shouting out in the hope of being engaged. "Call out twenty-one, Sir, that's me Sir," cries out one man. "Thirty-six did you say, Sir?" cries another. "Here I am, Sir, number eighteen, Sir," holloas a third. "Take your baggage up, Sir. I'm thirteen, Sir," shouts a fourth. "Carry your bag, Sir, number twenty-four, Sir, take it for sixpence, Sir," bawls out a fifth in tones fit to split the drum of your ear. "Get out of the way, it's my turn; that man aint no business here, and the gen'lman looked at me, didn't you, Sir?" roars a sixth. "No he didn't," says another, a very roguish looking chap, who was standing out of the rank and nearly up to his knees in water, " his honour winked at me." And so it goes on until the captain or the policeman interferes in your behalf, and scatters these hungry officials right and left. Not only unpleasant to be so bothered, but to have insult added to injury, by being told that you indulge in the vulgar habit of winking—it is really too bad. But Hobbler did not mind it; in fact having only a small carpet-bag with him, I think he rather liked the fun. Moreover he was again revolving in his mind what a charming thing it was to land, and not be subjected to that very unpleasant inquisition—the Custom House.

Now Hobbler only spent a few days in Guernsey; but, nevertheless, he was enabled, by the aid of a four wheeler, to see most of the places of attraction in the island, and as was his usual good fortune he found several agreeable companions ready to join him.

This makes a very inexpensive amusement, for you can hire a horse and chaise for the greater part of the day for six shillings. This between four people is not very extravagant for a day's amusement and instruction; though doubtless to the good pedestrian even this can be dispensed with, and a still greater amount of gratification be derived. So thought Hobbler, and so thinking, his mind reverted to the days when he could have tramped the Island of Guernsey round in one day; for previous to his illness, he had been what would be termed rather a great walker. But he was not much given to grumbling, so he only thought of those days, he did not talk about them; and not being able to walk, he was very thankful that carriage hire was so cheap, as to allow him to ride. Well then he rode, and who would not do so, situated as he was? Reader, would not you? Always provided you have the chance. But let us start fair, and it is but right to say a few words about the capital of the island, St. Peter's Port, before we ramble into the country; for in these days of centralisation, when according to the theory of some men, who are styled the men of progress, the towns are all in all, and the country but as nothing, it will not do to put the cart before the horse—though if our own individual views were expressed, we would candidly confess that we sometimes think it a very pleasing variation in the usual monotonous routine. However, though Paris may not be quite all France;

and London, Manchester and Birmingham are certainly not yet all England; and St. Peter's Port not quite all Guernsey, though doubtless a great part of it, I will be orthodox, and so to the town.

The town of St. Peter's presents rather a curious appearance on approaching it from the sea, from its being built on the side of a hill. On its extreme right, at about a mile distance, is a battery of some strength. On its extreme left, and elevated on lofty cliffs, is a very high column raised to the memory of Sir John Doyle, one of the former governors of the island. Immediately in its front is Castle Cornet, a short distance from the shore, the harbour and piers lying between. The town rises abruptly from the water's edge, the upper parts being some hundreds of feet above the level of the sea, and being reached by very precipitous streets, or flights of many steps. The streets are of a very narrow and intricate character, and the one boasting the name of the High Street is a thoroughfare of a most ordinary description, and must have received its name more from the fact of its running up a very steep hill, than from any pretensions it can put forth as to its superiority over its fellows. It is true that the best shops are here ; and, hence,

Hobbler supposed its high title. The esplanade is altogether of a different character. The side next the sea is not built upon, and the road is a good width, with the exception of one part, which will probably soon be improved, and made to correspond with the rest.

Castle Cornet, as I have said, very much reminds one of Elizabeth Castle, at St. Heliers, standing on a rock some distance out to sea, though now it is nearly connected with the land by the new pier. This castle is a fine pile of buildings and stands up in grand relief, when viewed from the shore, either at morning or evening twilight. It is well worth a visit, and has some history attached to it. In the time of the Commonwealth, this castle was most gallantly held against the Parliamentary forces, and did not capitulate until it was found that further resistance was useless.

The harbour and piers of St. Peter's are well worthy of notice. Here there are most extensive works going on. The old harbour and piers are of a very limited character, but the new ones, when completed, will be not only commodious, but also a great ornament to the town. There are two splendid granite piers in course of construction, which, when finished, it is hoped will be of sufficient length to enable the steam boats to come alongside at all times of the tide, instead of as at present landing their passengers in small boats.*

Like St. Heliers, St. Peter's has very few handsome buildings. There are some fine barracks on the heights, and a very fine college on the north-eastern hill, called Elizabeth College. This latter is a handsome building of the castellated style, built in the reign of Queen Elizabeth, after whom it was named.

There is a curious old church on the Esplanade, but the ecclesiastical buildings of this town, like all its other buldings, with a very few exceptions, are of a very inferior order. Indeed, there is no use disguising the fact, that one must not visit the Channel Islands in the expectation of seeing any beauties of architecture (saving always that of nature's work, which is magnificent), for not only is there a great dearth of handsome buildings, but one does not even find here that quaint style of architecture, that you would be led to expect you

* Since writing the above, the works of the harbour have been so far completed, that the steamers are generally enabled to go alongside the piers.

might see in a place in such near proximity to the province of Normandy, where one meets with so much that is picturesque and interesting. I might add that the private buildings of this island are rather superior to those in Jersey.

The markets of St. Peter's are not equal to those of the capital of the sister island, with the exception of the fish market, which is perhaps one of the finest and best supplied in Europe. It is a fine, lofty building of great length, down each side of which are the stalls. Every stall has a marble slab, over which a constant supply of pure water is flowing, and the fish look as fresh as if they were in the sea; and the fishwomen also look very fresh and blooming, and with their Norman caps of snowy whiteness, add much to the general effect. It is really quite a treat to walk through this market on Saturday, and see the splendid display of fish of all kinds, and the beautifully clean and tempting manner in which they are laid out. There is a good supply every day in the week, but Saturday is the great day, not only to see the fish and the picturesque vendors thereof, but also to see the ladies, who on that day frequent the markets in large numbers, and elegantly attired.

Of course, the other sex very naturally follow, and so the fish market becomes a fashionable promenade. Fish, owing to its abundance in this market, may be, of course, procured very cheap.

Before quitting the town, it were well to say a word about the hotel where Master Hobbler ensconced himself during his stay in this island.

The two principal houses here, are said to be the Yacht in High Street, and Gardner's Hotel on the Esplanade; but our traveller went to the British in High Street, then kept by a Mrs. Marquis, where he found his quarters very comfortable, his living very excellent, and his hostess very kind and attentive. The coffee room of this hotel was charmingly situated. Entering by a door in the High Street, which runs parallel to the Esplanade, but up a steep hill, you go through a long narrow passage to this coffee room, where you find yourself in a very capital sized room, with a window taking in the whole width of the Esplanade frontage, for you look down upon that street, which lies some twenty or thirty feet below you.

The harbour lies at your feet, and, with all its shipping, forms a very lively foreground. Castle Cornet is a short distance beyond, looking like some grim old fortress just risen out of the ocean. About four miles off are the Islands of Herm and Jethou, Serk about seven, and Jersey in the distance twenty miles away. This view, on a bright summer's day when the sea is sparkling in the glory of a noon day sun, is most charming, and the verdant isles, scattered on the ocean, look like beauteous emeralds set in glittering diamonds. For a sea-view, this is perhaps the liveliest and most picturesque our traveller ever beheld from an hotel window.

But we will take our country trip now, and first let us have a look at the most uninteresting parts of the island, saving the most beautiful, like children do the tit-bits of their meals, until the last.

Starting eastward from St. Peters, the coast presents no particular features of interest. Some few miles from the town is St. Samsons, a town or a village, I hardly know which it is called, where an omnibus plies to. This omnibus, our traveller thought, was a great deal more fit to be called a cart, for it certainly more resembled that kind of vehicle, covered in, with doors and windows put to it, than an omnibus.

St. Samsons is a very ugly place, with a harbour, however, capable of containing vessels of some size. So the guide books say, but when our traveller visited it, it was low water; and low enough it was, and this harbour did not look like a harbour at all. Passing round the north-eastern parts of the island, the view is none of the finest. The country is flat and sterile, and in many places the roads are covered with sand, giving the whole neighbourhood a very desolate appearance. Much of the land in this part has only been reclaimed from the sea within the last few years. Rocks of a reddish colour are sprinkled about in all directions for some miles out to sea, and render this part of the coast very dangerous for navigation, and consequently very safe from invasion.

Cobo bay, in the north side of Guernsey, is a place of great resort, being within a drive of four miles of St. Peters, straight across the middle of the island. There is a famous little inn here, called the Cobo hotel, once very celebrated for its pancakes. Whatever it may have been celebrated for, Hobbler cannot certify, but he thinks that now it must be celebrated as the residence of one of the funniest old creatures he ever saw, in the shape of its landlady, Mrs. Mundey. This worthy old lady does not own to be old, and it is difficult to say what her age may be, she looks any age you like on the shady side of—well no matter what, it might be libellous, so I won't say. Her husband, who she calls Billy, is also probably not so old as appearances would lead one to imagine he was. Billy was dressed very smartly in blue coat, bright buttons, plum coloured waistcoat, and fancy trowsers; but mine hostess was attired in very simple costume, a dress of a light dust coloured cotton fabric, made very straight, no crinoline, but in the fashion of fifty years ago. The said dress looked as if it had been near the frying pan, and not far off the chimney, but this might only be fancy. Mine hostess was decidedly not pretty; I can't say what she might have been in her youthful days, but now her features were rather angular, and her complexion somewhat cadaverous; in fact she looked not very unlike the sound of her voice, just half a tone sharp.

Billy was ruddy and in good condition, but somewhat lacked expression, and his voice was perhaps something like himself, just half a tone flat. Now Billy, it appears, had been a fast man in his time. He had been a bon vivant and a jolly companion once, and felt it necessary, in the excess of sociability and conviviality, to indulge in large potations with the numerous guests who, a few years ago, frequented his house; and Billy's head, not being strong enough to withstand the inroads that such indulgences will at some time or other most assuredly make in such cases, has given way, that is to say, I am afraid he has become a sort of silly Billy, and his worthy spouse is constantly informing the visitors of this fact.

Now, as has been said, mine hostess was of a very eccentric turn of mind, but she was also possessed of a very kind disposition, and despite all her eccentricity, there was no disguising it. Well, pitying poor Hobbler's state of health, she immediately became very friendly, motherly, and patronising towards him, as well as very communicative. She related to him the above facts about poor Billy, as she called him, and said she, stroking his head (Billy's head, I mean, not Hobbler's), " Poor Billy was a very good fellow in his day, and a very good scholar too," she added, " and now cuts up beans beautifully. My dear boy," she said, addressing Hobbler, " Billy is a very good fellow still some times." Query, thought our traveller, if he is only fitted for cutting up beans. She further said that if Hobbler would come and stop at her house, she would make him very comfortable, and that he should live like a prince, for she was considered the best cook in the island. "Ain't I, Billy?" she asked of the poor, mild looking fellow. "Yee'es," said Billy, looking up from the beans. "And you will make the dear boy very comfortable, wont you Billy?" "Ye-ees," again responded Billy, once more raising his eyes from the vegetables that he was operating upon. She then made our traveller a present of some fine pears, for which she would not accept a farthing in payment, being rather indignant at the offer. "Poor Billy," she began, soliloquising; "Poor Billy, he was a good fellow once, but he ought to have been dead long ago."

Hobbler now began to think that things were growing serious, and that Billy might become jealous. Pistols, measured paces, and grim seconds, loomed unpleasantly in the distance, though to all appearance poor old Billy quietly acquiesced in the idea that he ought to have been dead long ago. With many protestations of kindness and affection, and another repetition of her words that "Billy ought to have been dead long ago," our traveller was allowed to depart. When next he goes that way, probably poor Billy may have paid the debt of nature, and then who can predict what might be the consequence, if again subjected to the fascinations of the widow Mundey and her pancakes. Here we must quit Cobo bay, having lingered there far too long; but we advise all visitors to Guernsey to go there, if it is only to see the funny landlady, whose fame is certainly very extensive, and not unmerited, both on account of the goodness of her cookery, and her kindness, as well as for the amusement which she can never fail to afford her visitors. Though Cobo bay is an uninteresting place, the ride to it from St. Peter's is one of the prettiest in the island.

Let us now take a journey in the other direction. Leaving the town in a westerly direction and ascending a very steep hill, the barracks and the monument to Sir John Doyle are passed, after which the road descends gradually to one of the prettiest spots in the island called Fermain bay. This is a very charming place, but our traveller·

after describing in rather a detailed manner all the principal bays of Jersey, does not think it necessary to go so fully into those of Guernsey, as in many respects there is a great similarity between them, though the Guernsey beauties are much fewer in number than those of the other island. The principal bays are Fermain, Petit Bot, Moulin, Huet, Rocquaine bay and Torteval, a visit to any one of which will amply repay the traveller for any trouble and fatigue he may incur in reaching them. All of them may be approached by small roads or lanes, winding along the sides of the hills, and gradually descending to the sea-shore, and all of them lie on the south and south-west of the island.

The views obtained through the openings in the hills in this part of Guernsey, are most picturesque, and the coast, at the particular places named above, is very grand, the shore rising to a great altitude in bold and rocky crags, in some places wild and barren in the extreme, in others surmounted by hills covered with grass or heather. Petit Bot is particularly beautiful, and the scenery of this bay surpasses perhaps that of any of the splendid bays of Jersey, though as a rule the scenery of the latter island very far outshines that of its neighbour, both in beauty and grandeur.

The gardens of Guernsey are very beautiful, and flowers of all kinds flourish most luxuriantly, even more so than in Jersey, and in some places the houses may be seen covered with fuschias and geraniums, and the parterres round St. Peter's Port generally present a most beautiful appearance, the various flowers being brought to a great state of perfection, much more labour being bestowed on them than in Jersey.

The general appearance, however, of this island is altogether different to that of its neighbour, and in comparison with it, is rather barren, there being an absence of those splendid orchards and arcades of fruit trees, as well as clusters of forest trees, which makes almost every part of the Island of Jersey so attractive to the tourist—who misses also here those charming lanes, with their verdant banks and hedges, through which you can ramble with such delight in the more southern island.

But though the traveller will not be so much struck by the scenery of Guernsey, as he is by that of Jersey, he will probably come to the conclusion that as far as the people are concerned, the former island would be the pleasanter of the two to reside in. The inhabitants are very fond of money, but the love of it does not take possession of the minds of men to the extent that it does in the sister island, neither does party spirit run so high. The Guernsey people have a patois of their own, as well as the English and French languages which latter are both spoken by the educated classes.

The folks here are very polite, and the upper classes more refined than those of Jersey. From the lower classes, especially the peasantry, one generally meets with a degree of civility and respect, which a resident of any length of time never looks for in Jersey, and consequently he is never disappointed, though perhaps a casual visitor may think differently.

The upper classes of Guernsey are decidedly in advance of their neighbours. And this is accounted for by many, not only by the fact of their being many more old families of respectability in the one island than the other, but also by a 'still more significant fact, and that is that Guernsey, alias its people, has long been addicted to travel, whereas Jersey has only lately taken to it; consequently the ideas of one people are more enlarged than those of the other. In proportion, however, to their greater amount of aristocratic birth and refinement, the Guernsey folks possess their due amount of pride, and classes and cliques figure in this island to perfection, though, as for this matter, the Jersey people are not by any means deficient.

Guernsey has a copper coinage of its own, French silver is current, and English gold. In Jersey they have their own copper coinage, thirteen pence to the shilling, English silver and English gold.

There is a great diversity of opinion among travellers as to which of the islands, Guernsey or Jersey, is the most picturesque. Of course everybody forms their own opinion, and retains it; but as far as our traveller's views are concerned, he gives his humble opinion that Guernsey is not to be compared in beauty to the sister island, at the same time he considers that it presents a never ending series of charming and delightful rambles, and he most strongly recommends every one who visits Jersey, or any of the other islands, never to dream of coming home again, until they have also paid a visit to the Island of Guernsey.

CHAPTER V.

THE ISLANDS OF SERK, HERM, JETHOU AND ALDERNEY, AND THE CASKET ROCKS.

Excursion to Serk.—The Voyage.—Neptune and Boreas at play, and the Steward at work.—Fair Venus in danger.—The parting glass.—Approach to the Island.—Harbour of Le Creux.—La Coupée and its story.—General description of the Island.—Herm and its tiny shells.—Melancholy incident.—Life and Death.—Jethou.—Alderney and its fortified works.—The Casket Rocks.

"THE sun is up, the lark is soaring," and the planet Venus, the bright morning star, and all the multitudinous hosts of heaven, have paled before the brighter light of old Sol. But not so the steamer Venus, which now appears on the scene, and with steam up seems to delight in its glorious reflections. With a full cargo of pleasure seekers, numbering among them Mr. Hobbler, she moves smoothly out of St. Heliers' harbour, and all on board rejoice at the gladness and brightness of the prospect.

Now they say that "pleasure is a term that often means pain," and perhaps this saying is never applied with greater truth than to an excursion to sea. Smoothly out of the harbour glides the vessel, but not smoothly does she glide on. "Tell me who your companions are, and I will tell you what you are," again to quote old proverbs. Well, old Neptune all the previous night had been keeping company with rude Boreas, and had accordingly caught some of the infection of his rude spirit, and was slightly inclined to be rude too, being a trifle ruffled in his temper this fine morning. And the beautiful Venus found herself fishing in troubled waters, so that many of the pleasure seekers, even ere her speed was fully attained, wished themselves again on shore. Not being able however, to gratify these wishes, comfortable berths to leeward, and a goodly array of basins became the order of the day.

Rough and rude were the waters that morning, as passing St. Brelades, (all beauteous in its sunny morning garb it appeared,) the steamer ploughed on through their foam-dashing billows, and each passenger received a fresh christening at the hands of the briny old sea god, old Sol standing sponsor, and looking down, with beams of glorious satisfaction on his bright visage, upon his godchildren, most of whom did not at all appreciate the attentions of either party. And now the steamer approaches the south-western point of the island, known as La Corbiere, a wild spot where the sea is ever restless; and here according to our traveller's anticipation, the strife of waters vented their full fury upon the beautiful goddess. The land, after that point was past, interposing itself between her and the boisterous waves, she found herself suddenly in smooth water. But it was a warm parting, something like the parting glass or stirrup cup used in Scottish festivities in years happily gone by, which if the previous potations had not taken effect, was sure to finish the addlement of what few senses its recipient might have left, for Neptune's parting glass that day was on a scale to put all previous libations quite into the shade, and the fair Venus staggered under the effects of such copious draughts. Whether he did it in exuberance of his spirits, or whether the poor thing of earth who controlled the movements of the laughing beauty put her too much into the eye of the windy god upon that half merry, half angry sea, it matters not; but sure it is, that watery god, raising his trident aloft, rushed on board that ship in all his vigorous majesty, and breaking right ahead rolled grandly over both bows in a broad stream, and washed the vessel in a complete torrent from stem to stern, knocking down in his fun two or three of fair Venus's passengers who stood at the head of the boat (like the Irishman who meets with a friend and for love knocks him down), and drenching every one within his reach. The point is however past, the sun is still shining gloriously, and old Neptune, satisfied with his morning escapade, looks bright and joyous, and calms his exuberant and ruffled spirits. Luckily he did so, for a few more such exhibitions of his prowess might possibly have sent the loving goddess and her attendant mortals to seek any further amusement and enjoyment among his fair friends the mermaids.

Serk now hove in sight, rising precipitately from its ocean bed, like a fragment of some large island cast from its parent soil by some vast convulsion of nature, or like a huge rock torn by a mighty giant's hand, and pitched into the middle of the sea.

Soon the island is reached, and the poor helpless mortals, whom Neptune's vagaries had laid prostrate for the greater part of this very pleasant and charming excursion began to hold up their heads, laughter mingling with the now subsiding sounds of a far more questionable and less pleasant character that had been heard throughout the morning; wetted garments were thrown aside, basins vanished from the scene, the vessel anchored off the romantic harbour on the south side of the island; all was again joy and gladness, and the steward was at peace.

But there was an exception to this brightened picture, in one poor unhappy lady, who appeared so perfectly prostrated by the effects of the rough sea, that she was obliged to be slung ashore in a hammock; and when the vessel left that afternoon, she was unable to return to it, and as our traveller afterwards heard, she never recovered from the shock, but sank from sheer weakness and exhaustion, and died the next day. A sad termination to a trip of pleasure, and one that makes us ponder how people who are subject to this terrible malady in such a form, can venture on the sea for a pleasure excursion.

The harbour to which I have alluded is called Le Creux, and our traveller thought that, without any exception, it was the wildest and most picturesque scene of the kind he had ever beheld. Land-locked in every sense of the word it is, three sides of it being shut in by perpendicular rocks rising to a height of two or three hundred feet above the sea, the fourth side closed up by a lofty wall running out at right angles from one of these rocky cliffs, merely leaving an opening for small vessels and boats to enter. Inside this secluded nook, your boat is run on the beach, for there is no other landing place; and when there, you find yourself apparently without the means of egress, except that by which you had obtained admission. But you discover at last that what had appeared at a distance only like the opening to some cavern, is in reality a tunnel through the rock, and leads to the interior of the island.

A cavern originally, no doubt it was, and nothing else; the only entrance to Serk in former times being by a precipitate flight of steps, or rather a succession of foot holes in the face of the rock, and a rope suspended from the top of the cliff, up which only the strong and nervous man could possibly climb.

After passing through the tunnel, the road winds up and up, until at last you find yourself at the top of the table land of the island, and somewhere about its centre.

Hobbler was fortunate enough to have on his visits to Serk fair companions, who tempted him, by their persuasions, to go on and on in search of the hotel, rather further than was compatible with his state of health and strength; but who can hesitate when fair lady leads the way? The hotels, for there were two of them, were at last discovered among the trees, and within very little distance of each other. They were, however, further from the landing-place than his friends had imagined, though really but a short distance for a person in good health to walk, perhaps three quarters of a mile.

Both these houses appear to be very comfortable, though the one kept by Mrs. Hazelhurst has decidedly the advantage in situation over the other. Our traveller went to the other one for the few hours he remained in the island, and was well satisfied with the accommodation he received there. Here he met some friends, by whom he was introduced to a medical gentleman, who had been some time resident in the island, and who strongly recommended him to remain there, as the most healthy one of all the group.

Serk is a most remarkable island, and decidedly the most romantic and wild of all the Islands of the Southern British Channel. As I have stated, it is like a large rock rising out of the ocean, nearly every part of its coast line ascending perpendicularly from the shore. It is a very small island, not any part of it being more than a mile and a half across, and its greatest length only about three and a half miles. The population is about seven hundred souls. There is a church here of a very primitive character, and surrounded by a garden teeming with the most luxuriant flowers, which latter are carried away in the season by handsful by the visitors, who seem to think that if any place, no matter what, is open for their inspection, they have the liberty to do as they please with its contents. This desecration of the dwelling place of the dead, for I cannot use any other words to describe the wanton act, is I am sorry to say generally perpetrated by the excursionists, mostly English people, for I do not believe the inhabitants of the island would be guilty of such a disgraceful act.

There are no villages in this island, the houses being dotted about in all directions, as if they had been built, and then pitched down just where the fancy of the owner prompted him, perfectly regardless of any formation of communities, such as are to be found in the larger islands, or frequently in England, in neighbourhoods with a very much smaller number of inhabitants in proportion to the size of the surrounding district.

Serk is altogether a charming place to the lover of the wild and magnificent in nature, for though the island is so small, the scenery is very grand, and had our traveller been sufficiently in possession of the use of his limbs, nothing would have delighted him more than remaining there for a week or two, and drinking in the health-giving breezes which, turn where you will, seem to meet you at every step you take.

This island, at a first view of it, would give you the idea of being all a table land, but it is not entirely so by any means; but is intersected by deep wooded romantic dells, through which flow several sweet little bubbling streams. These valleys are very richly beautiful, and contrast most admirably with the barren and rugged character of the coast scene in general.

Dixcart bay and valley are charming. Shut in by hills profusely clad with verdure, and teeming with brilliant and fragrant wild flowers, it is indeed a most enchanting spot.

Port Frey, Port du Moulin and Terrible bay are all well worth the traveller's inspection. Indeed the whole islands may be described as a delightful series of beautiful landscapes.

The great wonder however of Serk is the Coupée, a narrow ledge of rock, or bridge, connecting Great and Little Serk together; for I should state that the island is divided into two parts, which are only joined together by this narrow causeway.

This pathway which is about four hundred feet in length, is only a few feet broad, and being at an elevation of three or four hundred feet from the sea, on one side absolutely perpendicular, and on the other not very far removed from it, is a place that requires rather a steady head to cross it.

There is a funny tale told about this spot, concerning a man who lived in Little Serk, but who spent his evenings at a public-house in the larger island. He is said to have indulged rather freely in his evening potations, and not being always able to maintain so just an equilibrium as might be necessary to cross over this narrow bridge, he adopted the very curious test as to whether he possessed the required amount of sobriety, by walking along an old cannon which lay on the ground on the Great Serk side of the bridge. If he succeeded in walking over this gun, he was able to cross with safety; but if he tumbled off (which doubtless was very often) he laid there, until another experiment on the gun told him that his brains had sufficiently recovered their steadiness, to enable him to cross over the dangerous causeway. Truly there is a method in madness, so they say, and as drunkenness is a species of madness, this anecdote decidedly corroborates the old adage, for there was a considerable amount of method displayed by this island toper.

The cliffs are intersected by numerous caverns, and the effect of light and shade on the rocks is most beautiful; at sunset more especially so, when they appear in ever varying tints, and assume almost every shade of colour. Though the Island of

Serk is of such small dimensions, it must be allowed most certainly to bear away the palm in point of fine scenery from all the other islands, beautiful though those others be.

This little island is a sort of small kingdom in itself. It has its own little army in its militia, the colonel of which is the Seigneur of the island, and a kind of petty sovereign. It grows its own corn, and builds its own boats, is governed by its own laws, and altogether is a very independent sort of a place to live in; though it is somewhat to be doubted whether the inhabitants could get on altogether without supplies from the neighbouring islands.

Serk is an island that ought to be seen by every visitor to these parts, and the traveller in this neighbourhood who neglects to go there, misses a sight which he may journey many a long mile before he finds anything like its equal.

Like all the other islands, this one has a great store of legend attached to it; but I cannot possibly enter into them here as it would swell my book to too great a bulk, but to those who would like to peruse some of the fabulous tales connected with it, and I can assure my readers they are of a most romantic character, I again recommend them to the guide book by Mr. Rooke. Our traveller visited Serk on two occasions, and on both of them enjoyed himself exceedingly. Though very fatigued, he managed, through the kind offices of the medical gentleman before alluded to, to procure a seat in the only vehicle that is let out for hire in the island, and though the roads are none of the smoothest, he arrived safe and sound at the little harbour, which the steamer quitted about four o'clock in the afternoon, reaching Jersey before dark. It is as well perhaps to add that being in good company and not being subject to sea sickness, the day had no drawbacks to our traveller.

On another day in the autumn, a little later in the season, but just such a beautiful one as that described in the beginning of this chapter, Hobbler found himself again on board that fast and favourite steamer Venus, which was about to pay a visit to the two smaller Islands of Herm and Jethou, which lie within a very few miles of Serk, on the side most distant from Jersey. The passage between this latter island and Serk was much of the usual description, and the vessel arrived off the harbour of Le Creux about ten o'clock in the morning. Here she landed about half her passengers. The passage between Serk and the other islands is rather of a dangerous character, and requires a good knowledge on the part of the captain of the particular rocks to be avoided and the currents to be encountered, in order to secure a safe journey in any weather, but especially so in a rough sea.

Now, this was the only excursion to Herm this year, and consequently going so seldom, the captain of the Venus was not particularly well acquainted with the navigation. This difficulty was, however, got over by taking on board at Serk an old fisherman from Herm, who acted as pilot, in whom it is no great disrespect to the captain of the steamer to say, Hobbler felt much more confidence, as he appeared perfectly conversant with those waters, which the captain certainly did not, as he was heard enquiring whether after leaving Serk, he should go eastward or westward. Doubtless he could have gone either way, but still the sea not being very smooth that day, it was much more pleasant to be under the charge of a man who had spent the greater part of his life on that coast, than under that of one who appeared to be somewhat ignorant of it.

The islands were safely reached, and the steamer cast anchor between them about mid-day. The landing place was of a most primitive character, being on the rugged rocks, and a rugged path it was too after you had landed; and had not our traveller been supported by a strong arm, he would have been unable to reach the shore, but must, most certainly, have returned on board the steamer, without fulfilling the principal object he had in coming to Herm, namely the procuring some of the tiny shells for which this island is so celebrated.

Herm is a very small island, about three or four miles in circumference. It has two small hotels, but it is quite certain that they cannot be supported by the inhabitants, who do not muster one hundred strong, but must rather depend upon the visitors, who in the summer time come over in large numbers from Guernsey, which is not four miles distant from it. Indeed, when standing on the beech at Herm, St. Peter's Port appears but a very little way off, and one could more fancy that one was looking across a broad river, than a channel of the ocean.

Yes, and a very pretty river too, for being a very bright day, the view of the island of Guernsey from this spot was particularly fine, indeed as good a one as you can procure any where.

A ramble through Herm will amply repay the traveller for the trouble of a day's excursion there, though at the same time it must be added that after viewing the other islands in this neighbourhood, both Herm and Jethou appear very tame.

The scenery is wild and rocky, but a detailed description of it would not be interesting to the reader, after that of the other islands.

The shells which so many people come here in search of are a great attraction. They are of a very diminutive character, though doubtless at some period, large shells have abounded on this coast; for a mile of the shore at high water mark, for about a yard wide, is a mass of shell dust, not sand nor gravel, but positively for some depth nothing but broken shells, ground by the incessant action of the waves into small particles. It is among this dust that the small shells so much prized are found, and it has been asserted by some authorities in such matters, that most of the shells that are found on the various sea-coasts of the world, are found here in miniature. Hobbler brought away with him a large bag of this shell dust, from which he afterwards extracted quantities of very beautiful shells, some of them so small that they were hardly to be discovered with the naked eye, and he has no doubt but that with the aid of a microscope they might be found by thousands upon thousands of such a diminutive size, as only to be detected by a very strong magnifying power.

Jethou, the sister island to Herm, is a place of no note whatever, having only one house upon it, and being little else than a large rabbit warren. The passage between the two islands is of a very narrow and dangerous nature.

Before quitting these islands, our traveller wishes to relate the occurrence of a most melancholy incident, which though not connected with his visit there, for it occurred when he was in Guernsey, still as it relates to Herm, it is not quite out of place to mention it here.

On a beautiful bright morning during one of his visits to Guernsey, Hobbler was taking a stroll before breakfast in order to court an appetite for that meal, when he observed a small sailing vessel, with about a dozen people in it, on the point of starting for an excursion to Herm. There were folks of both sexes on board, some old and some young; and there were glad and merry hearts in that boat, as dancing in the merry sunshine, she sped her lively course across the sparkling sea.

Our traveller watched her and her gay cargo, as with canvass spread to catch the favouring breezes of that fine morning, they gradually disappeared from his view and entered the little strait that separates Herm from Jethou. And he went home to his morning meal, and thought to himself what a merry party he had seen, and how by that time they were disporting themselves on the sandy beach or bramble-covered hills of Herm, or how they were hunting for the tiny shells. And Hobbler went forth with his friends to his day's amusement, exploring some of the richest of nature's beauties, as displayed in the Island of Guernsey. And the day had well nigh waned, night had begun to close in upon the scene, man had ceased from his labours, and the pale moon had risen on the earth. Our traveller had returned to his hotel, and was spending the evening in pleasant converse with his friends, having well nigh forgotten that lively party that he had seen quit the beach in the morning so full of life and spirits.

Where were they now? Had they spent a happy day, and had they returned to a happy home at night? All had perhaps passed a day of enjoyment and merriment, and some had returned to their homes, but not all.

Towards night came gloomy rumours of a boat being upset on the treacherous waters that surround these islands in all directions. Rumour soon ripened into sad reality, and before long it was known all over St. Peters, that that great enemy of man, who so often steps in to mar his brightest hopes, and so often crosses his path when least expected, and who in a moment converts the full spring time of pleasure and enjoyment into the seared and autumnal time of mourning and sorrow—in a word it was but too soon known, that grim death had in a few short hours been rife among the merry party, that the boat had been capsised, and four of those joyous beings who had quitted that shore a few hours before so full of life, had returned to them joy no longer beaming in their eyes, laughter no longer issuing from their throats and lighting up their faces, but cold, stiff, and inanimate corpses.

Truly, as some of our moralists would say, such was the morning and such the night. The former all gladness, joy, hope, sunshine and vigorous life—the latter sorrow, mourning, darkness and death. This accident cast a sad gloom over all the town, and our traveller retired to his bed sad and serious, reflecting on the uncertainty of human life, which like the grass of the field to-day is, and to-morrow is cast into the oven.

I stop not to enquire into the cause of this melancholy accident, but pass on to the conclusion of this chapter.

The steamer returned in safety from Herm, touching again at the romantic island of Serk, which in the subdued light of the fast fading day looked more grand and picturesque than ever, and arrived at St. Heliers in the dusky hour of twilight.

This was the last of Hobbler's excursions.

There remains one more island to be noticed, which perhaps my readers will think ought to have been passed under observation before the smaller ones last named, and that is Alderney; but as our traveller did not go there, he has very little to say about it from personal observation, having only seen it from a distance. From all he has read and heard of it, he thinks it must be a very uninteresting place as compared to Jersey, Guernsey or Serk. But it is much talked of just now on account of the prodigious government works that are being carried on there, in the shape of a harbour of refuge and naval station, and from its position, commanding as it does the important harbour of Cherbourg on the French coast, it may some day become a place of some consequence. The great, and in fact the only inducement for the tourist to visit Alderney, will be to view these extensive fortifications. The only town in Alderney is St. Anne's.

The Casket Rocks of which it is usual to speak when writing of the Channel Islands, are the nearest points of land to the English coast. There is little to say about them, but that on these rocks are erected three light-houses, which stand as the watchful sentinels of the Channel to warn the mariner off their inhospitable shores, to tell him of his whereabouts.

The chief attractions in the islands of the

Southern British Channel have been passed under review, and we will now suppose Hobbler returned to his Jersey home, after having seen all the lions described in the last three chapters. The next chapter will find him in a new character at his quiet and comfortable retreat at Bouley.

CHAPTER VI.

THREE MONTHS' RETIREMENT AT BOULEY.

Hobbler returned to his Jersey home, appears in a new character.—Cincinnatus.—My bed-room.—Our kitchen.—He studies domestic economy.—Turns cook, and goes a marketing.—A Thunderstorm.—The Fêtes at Cherbourg.—Hobbler's Dream of the Future.—Atlantic Telegraph. — The Comet. — Conclusion of the Season.—Harvest.—Fern Cutting.—Vraic Gathering.—Florence Nightingale.—The Ladies of Bouley.—Adieu to Bouley.

How delightful it is after the cares and troubles of public life, to retire into the sweet enjoyment of domestic and rural life. There was a certain old gentleman of whom I recollect reading when I was a boy, by the name of Cincinnatus, who after defeating the enemies of his country and having done a vast deal of public good, retired from the busy world and took to domestic pursuits, and was rather fond of his garden. "What's that that roars so loud and thunders in the index?" I dare say my readers will exclaim. Is it possible that he is going to compare his hero with the great Roman warrior. Most certainly not—I never dreamed of such a thing, I only wish to shew that one principle may apply to different objects, though of course in different degrees.

Now if a great man like Cincinnatus could find so much enjoyment in the retirement into rural and domestic life, leaving as he did all his honours behind him, hiding the glory of his achievements in obscurity, and foregoing all pretensions to public adulation, and that too in the very prime and vigour of his life—how much more delightful must it be to a poor crippled invalid, who had no honours to lose, and no glory to obscure, and who at the age of life when man is in his prime, very much resembled a good ship, that numbering but a small amount of years in its age has yet encountered such severe gales that it has been tried all but to foundering, and requires such a lengthened period of docking to put her right again, that the query is whether she will ever be fit for service any more; how much more delightful, I say, must it be to him, to find the sweet and invigorating repose of country life, than it was even to the great Roman general.

And he found that repose in his solitary dwelling on the Jersey sea coast, where I will now suppose that he has arrived, and again adopted the primitive and unsophisticated habits of rustic life.

Returned from his travels then, Hobbler became quite a domesticated animal at his house on the lone sea-coast of Bouley, and quite revelled in his little snuggery up among the beams and tiles of the old fashioned building. "My bedroom," that is to say Hobbler's, was in its way rather a curiosity. It had been constructed on what had been once a large landing, on the top or attic floor of the house, and somewhat resembled the cabin of a ship, being boarded all round, as well as being ceiled in the same manner, except the side nearest the road, which had a charming little window in the slant of the roof, which said window was propped open with an iron, and something like the traps that boys make with five bricks to catch unwary birds. This apartment was not very spacious, but nevertheless very snug and comfortable, and our traveller felt a great contempt for the man who could not be comfortable therein. There was a glorious old fashioned kitchen on the ground floor, the windows of which looked on to the sea. Now there were sundry parlours where our traveller could sit if he liked it, but as the season advanced and the visitors decreased, he did not like it, and I am reluctantly compelled to confess that he was more often found in this said kitchen ; for our traveller was not fond of solitary confinement, and moreover, he was somewhat of a curious turn of mind, and thought of entering himself as a student of domestic economy. I may as well add that " the kitchen" of a country inn is a totally different place to that of a town one, being a place where very frequently only the privileged are admitted ; and, besides all this, "our kitchen" at Bouley was a very sociable place, though if the truth must be told, our traveller was often in the way, and doubtless, had he not been an invalid, he would have received the due reward that his inquisitiveness merited. But our kitchen is now, alas, no more, and only lives in history, and in the memory of those who have partaken of the good fare that has issued from that good old fashioned cookery, being now supplanted by a modern cuisine.

His first studies, or his first practical demonstration of his presumed domestic knowledge (for I much fear that he began the practical, before he had learned the theoretical) was in cooking.

He fancied he could cook. What a low taste! what a vulgar fancy! I dare say some of you will exclaim—not quite sure of that, "friend of mine." Our hero might have had some visions of the Colonies, or London Chambers floating before his eyes where such an accomplishment is very useful.

Besides, great men have descended to be cooks, and great cooks have become great men. Did not that worthy physician, old Kitchener, write a cookery book? And did not the great cook Soyer become a literary character? and will not both of them live in history, to say nothing of the wonderful Mrs. Glass? Well then, Hobbler turned practical cook, and a rare cook he was. He thought he should be great at it; but he has confessed to me that he is fearful that nobody would engage him professionally, as somehow the fates appeared to be banded together against the proper development of his cuisine acquirements.

Yes, alas, it was so. He often found that in

doing a roast it was done to a cinder; in trying his hand at a boil, he discovered he had failed to put any water in the saucepan, the said saucepan being saved from destruction by a sort of miracle; that in performing a fry, the frizzling article would jump out of the frying pan into the fire; that in cooking an egg, it did occasionally tumble on to the floor and most probably break; and that in executing a toast, the bread invariably flirted with the bars and made its appearance in deep mourning; and in making—but no matter. What of all this? "accidents will happen in the best regulated families," they say, and doubtless will occur to the best of cooks. If the egg would not stand straight, how could he make it? The joke of Columbus was too stale for him to attempt an imitation. If the fry would tip up, that was a circumstance that could not be guarded against, for then the old proverb would not have been verified, and old proverbs are very true at times. If the roasting jack, or the chain, or the string, or any other article to which the roast was attached would stand still, how could it be avoided? Perpetual motion has not been discovered in cooking more than anything else. And if the bread would kiss the bars when toasted, it must not be blamed; it did not like this constant roasting or being under fire for so long a time, so I supposed turned black in the face with the warmth of its feelings. Perhaps it was a little wrong not to put some water in the saucepan, but still a good saucepan ought to be made to stand fire. And therefore the blame must lie principally at the door of the egg, or the fry, or the roast, or the toast, or the boiled, which had the perversity to be done as they were not wanted to be done; or the fire that would burn, or smoke, or frizzle when it was not required to do anything of the same sort. However, there is no fighting against a combination of adverse circumstances, and so Hobbler abdicated his position and resigned his cookship. Some folks had the impudence to say that he had mistaken his vocation; but it is always the case in this world in whatever you undertake, success ensures greatness, and failure brings obloquy. So singing a long farewell to all his greatness, he abdicated the grate.

His next escapade in the domestic world was rather a funny one, and certainly, considering the boldness of the attempt, did not meet with the success it deserved. But this is always the fate of genius. In the plentitude of his conceit (for I really fear he had become very conceited) he fancied he could do anything he tried, and so one day, for amusement, he thought he would turn laundry-maid for the nonce, and began crimping, or goffering, or performing some operation of a crinkly nature on the first fancy article that presented itself, probably mine hostess' best lace cap; when, lo! at the very first twist of the tongs or irons, he burnt a piece clean out of the aforesaid fancy article, and did the same kind turn for one of his own fingers. This soon took the conceit out of him; and in this business, I suppose that every body will return a verdict of served him right, in which verdict I presume, also, that he cannot help but concur.

And he took to gardening, but then his spine being a little out of the perpendicular, he did not find it agreeable. And he found he could not copy Cincinnatus, especially as he did not expect to be called off his work to attend to the cares of state.

And many other funny things he did at that old house, but as he did not pay any premium for his education in domestic economy, he does not feel at liberty to reveal all he did, and what he learnt, during his gratuitous household education. But his chief amusement was "going a marketing." Twice or thrice a week our traveller was to be seen jogging along the road leading to St. Heliers in a four-wheeler, belonging to mine host, accompanied by one of mine host's sons or daughters; and not very long after, they were to be seen perambulating the various markets described in the first chapter of this book.

And then what a learned man Hobbler became. He could tell you the price of bread and of meat, which he found much the same as in England; of butter which was better and much cheaper; of tea which he saw about two shillings per pound, and coffee one shilling, little more than half the price that they are in our country; sugar, also, and all kinds of grocery, very much cheaper than in the mother-country, owing of course to their being imported into Jersey duty free. To the poultry market also he went, and to the fish market. The produce of the first he found cheap, and the latter dear. And in these markets they bought ducks, and geese, and fowls; and soles, salmon, (very small quantity of the latter, however, it being rarely to be got under two shillings the pound) lobsters, crabs (ordinary crabs and spider crabs, funny looking animals) John Dorey, red and grey mullet, snipe fish (with green bones), and lots too numerous for me to mention, as well as garden stuff of all sorts, which is cheap and good. And then our traveller amused himself by rousing the people up a little, for it must be told that the tradespeople of St. Heliers are rather dilatory in their movements ; at any rate they do not move so fast as their promises would imply, being rather given to say that things are going directly, when they have not the slightest intention of sending them for an hour or two, or perhaps they protest they are already gone, when they are quietly reposing in their shops. But it is too bad to pick out the St. Heliers' tradesman as being addicted to a different standard of truth in business, to what they would practice out of it. I am fearful that it has generally become too much the fashion in business to say one thing and mean another. But let them pass.

After the purchases were made, our traveller and his companions would jog home again, and always on arriving at the top of the hill he used to think that this pretty bay looked prettier than ever. And often when our traveller journeyed into town, he went to visit some kind friends to whom he had been introduced on his arrival in the island, and with whom he had established a close intimacy, and from whom he was always sure to receive a warm and friendly greeting. Many and kind were the attentions that he received from these friends; and should these pages ever meet their eyes, he would beg them to believe that all their good and sympathising attentions towards the sick man, attentions such as warm and tender-hearted women (for these friends were ladies) alone know how to bestow, are stored away in the deepest and most sacred recesses of a grateful heart.

But, alas! one of them can never read these pages, for she is gone to that bourne from whence no traveller returns. She has gone to a premature grave, cut off in the flower of her age, and in the midst of a career of much usefulness; her loss being deplored, not only by our traveller who knew so well by experience her good and amiable qualities, but also beyond doubt by all who had the pleasure to be acquainted with that excellent, generous, and unselfish young lady. But she is gone where she will receive her reward.

I need hardly ask the kind and sympathising reader to pardon the exhibition of feeling that prompts our traveller to stop for a moment the course of his narrative, in order that he may drop a tear of gratitude and sorrow over the grave, as well as pay a slight tribute of respect to the memory of a kind, esteemed, and much lamented friend, who contributed much by her lively disposition and goodness of heart to sooth and cheer the weary hours of his pilgimage in search of health.

And so time passed away; but there was one sight which our traveller had long wished to see, and for which he had longed in vain, for many weeks—and that was a thunder-storm, which he fancied must be a very grand sight on that wild and rocky coast. But it came at last, though only once during his long stay at Bouley; and awful and majestic it was when it did come.

It was midnight, after a sultry August day. The family had all retired to rest; but our traveller found the air, which was highly charged with electricity, too heavy and oppressive to sleep. So he sat him down at his funny little window to watch the approach of the expected tempest.

Dark masses of cloud gathered in the horizon, and gradually spread themselves over the face of the whole heavens like a ponderous black curtain. An unusual and unnatural stillness pervaded the atmosphere, together with an extraordinary feeling of oppression, which are almost always the precursors of storms, and which stillness was only disturbed by the occasional soughing of a gloomy puff of wind passing by; a sort of avant courier of the mighty blasts that were so soon to follow.

"A boding silence reigns, dread thro' the dun expanse,
Save the dull sound, that from the mountain, previous to the storm,
Rolls o'er the muttering earth."

Faint flashes of lightning gave notice of the approach of the storm. These soon became more vivid, and succeeded each other with greater rapidity. The clouds became of a more opaque character, the wind began to howl most dismally, and the thunder, at first very distant, came rapidly rolling on, increasing in volume of sound and grandeur every minute. Onward and onward it rolled, nearer and nearer sounded heaven's stupendous artillery. Peal succeeded peal, and echo upon echo reverberating from hill to hill and from rock to rock, swelled out their mighty tones, until they became one tremendous and ceaseless roar. The clouds gave out an incessant fire, which shooting its forked streaks athwart the skies in all directions, often passed into the ocean, as if in defiance of its fire-quenching properties. Sheet upon sheet of flame leaped forth from those dark clouds, until all the firmament of heaven appeared in one prodigious blaze. The wind now roused to fury was roaring a tremendous blast, and flying upon its hurricane wing, lashed the ocean into a frenzied foam, resembling some vast boiling cauldron, and then both united, hurled themselves madly upon the wild and rocky shore.

For a moment the elemental strife was stayed, and all was intense calmness, and intense darkness. The hills, the sea, and even the distant coast of France had been visible under the bright illuminations of the lightning's ceaseless flash, but they were now buried in a profound gloom. It was, however, but a momentary lull in this battle of the elements, which was in reality fast approaching its culminating point. It was but a treacherous pause, during which they were gathering up all their forces, which in one united phalanx they were now about to hurl upon that lonely dwelling by the sea-shore of Bouley. The lull was of but short duration, and then the tempest broke forth with redoubled fury.

Rude was the onslaught, and terrific the shock that that poor old house had to encounter. The lightnings burst from all quarters of the heavens in one continued stream of liquid blue fire, the intensity of which seemed to permeate every crevice in the house, and appeared as if it would set the neighbouring hills on fire; the thunder broke upon the seemingly devoted roof with a terrific crash, that caused the whole fabric to tremble and quake beneath its mighty vibrations, as if it were about to crumble into pieces. The winds striving to make themselves heard above the awful din of the thunders roar, sent forth their raging blasts, and shook the poor old tenement, as if they would scatter it like chaff to the four winds of heaven; and the flood gates of the skies hitherto pent up, were now loosed, and with the sound of the rushing torrent, the rain descended on its roof as if it would have swept everything before it, and bury the house and all the dwellers therein in the deep bosom of the ocean.

The storm was now at its height, and for awhile it raged with a fearful violence; and during this awful combination of the elements in wrathful antagonism against this little speck of earth, it seemed as if the building, the island, yea, the great globe itself, and all that it inherits would dissolve, " and like the baseless fabric of a vision, leave not a wrack behind."

But it passed by, and left the old house and all its inhabitants uninjured. The fury of the tempest was spent. The lightning became less vivid and less frequent in its flashes, the thunder rolled away in the distance, the windows of heaven were again closed, the watery deluge subsided, the stormy winds abated their fury, black night and the cloudy curtain that had obscured the bright lamps of heaven passed away like a scroll, and the elemental strife was all over.

The day dawned, and thinking of the grandeur and magnificence of the scene he had witnessed, and reflecting on the insignificance of man when opposed to the elements if roused to anger, he fell asleep.

And when he rose in the morning what a change of scene was there.

Excepting that the rain had left the impress of its torrent course in the deep furrows it had ploughed in the sides of the hill, who would have known or thought, that but a few short hours before there had been such a terrific conflict of the elements raging around? Now all was calm and peaceful. The rude winds were hushed, the rushing torrent was stayed, and gentle zephyrs played upon the face of the earth; the sea was calm and placid, the sun shone with exquisite brightness, and refreshed nature reeked with joy and gladness.

While Hobbler was at Bouley, there was a great talk about the approaching fêtes at Cherbourg to commemorate the opening of the docks there, the foundations of which had been laid by Napoleon the First, and which were now about to be inaugurated by grand doings, at which the Emperor Napoleon the Third was to officiate, assisted by the Queen of Great Britain. Our traveller had several invitations to go there and see these mighty doings, but the state of his health would not allow him to think of it. So he did not see them, though within sound and also within sight of some part of the ceremony, for the fireworks were distinctly visible, though perhaps more than thirty miles off, and the grand salute which was fired upon the Emperor's arrival, was very audible.

It was late one evening in the month of August, when the birds had ceased their sweet melodies, and the sun had sank to his rest, the western sky still teeming with the refulgent light of his departing glory, that our traveller was sitting upon the rocky shore enjoying the sweet calm of evening's repose—when suddenly, far away in the distance over the coast of France, there arose a bright flash of light succeeded by a dull booming sound as of far off explosions. Brighter and brighter grew those flashes, louder and louder swelled that rumbling sound, and then they both died away altogether.

The inauguration of these mighty works of man, the construction of which had spread over a space of more than fifty years was consummated, the fêtes were over. This gigantic fortress, the future terror of the world, from whose vast harbours were

THE CHANNEL ISLANDS. 193

to issue fleets that should dictate to all opposing powers was complete.

And as the faint light of the distant illumination died away, night resumed his dominion, and all was darkness save the soft starlight of an autumn's eve.

Thinking of Cherbourg and its destiny, Hobbler fell a musing, and then he dreamed.

HOBBLER'S DREAM.

Falling into a reverie, I dreamed, and in my dream the distant shores of the Continent of Europe appeared to approach nearer and nearer to me, and my view became more and more extended over those far off countries. I saw, as it were, all the nations of that part of the world spread out like a map at my feet.

And what did I see, as I gazed upon these various countries, and gazed also into their future history? For years appeared to pass in quick review before me as well as nations.

I saw beautiful and broad lands as e'er the eye of man lighted upon. There was the mountain and the flood. Beautiful meandering streams were there, and sweet smiling pastures. Mighty rivers of torrent force, rising amidst snow-capped mountains; and peaceful valleys, ever verdant and joyous; gentle undulating hills, clothed with laughing vineyards, and merry cornfields ripe unto the harvest, sparkling in the sunshine, and reeking with plenty—all were displayed in that grand prospect, and all attested the wondrous bounty of nature's great Master. There also was the bustling town and ever active city; and the quiet country village, and tree embosomed hamlet were not wanting in that wide scene. And through all these vast dominions I saw man going forth to his labour, whether to toil at his pen in the towns, or at his plough in the fields, whether to labour with his hands in his factory, or with his brains in his study, or to take his pleasure in drinking in the rich draughts of all inspiring nature midst her wondrous beauties—I saw them all going forth in the sweet hope of reaping the reward of all their toils in happiness and peace, and rejoicing in the Giver of all good.

And this was sunshine, and this was peace.

But as I gazed, "a change came o'er the spirit of

my dream;" the character of that fair and peaceful prospect was transformed. A dark cloud had long been gathering in the realm of France, which had gradually spread its gloom over all Europe, thickening and thickening, until at last surcharged beyond all power of retention, it burst, and dreadful was the bursting thereof.

And what was this cloud that was now to discharge its rude torrents o'er all these lately smiling hills and plains?

I saw no longer man going to his peaceful labour or taking his pleasure; I saw no longer a peaceful scene at all, but in its stead an unending scene of darkness and of strife.

All the great hosts of Europe were gathered together for evil; for the love of war had taken possession of the souls of men, and nation was fighting against nation, and kingdom against kingdom. Smiling fields and plenteous harvests had been swept away, and devastation reigned in their place; meandering rivers, and glassy lakes sparkled no longer in the glorious sunshine, but ran red with the blood of contending nations. I saw the mightiest kingdoms of the earth banded together against one another, and all the great despotisms of the world were striving for supremacy in order to establish one universal thraldom.

There floated the mighty eagles of France, of Austria, of Russia, of Prussia with the flags of all the minor powers of Europe. All entered the lists on one side or the other. There were blended the Protestant, the Roman Catholic, and the Mohammedan banners, and the Crescent and the Cross waved side by side in this struggle for power and existence. Some were contending for universal sovereignty, some perhaps for a smaller aggrandisement, and some for very life. Liberty was the watchword with all, but alas in how few cases was it aught but a mockery. Power and ambition should have been the cry, if the leaders in this struggle had been honest.

Foremost in these fields of blood came forth with almost resistless force the mighty hosts of Gallia; and who should stay the torrent of her gigantic power. Madly and wildly she rushes on.

Imperial Austria feels the shock, and bends beneath the force of her terrific onslaughts. Mighty Russia retires from the conflict into her almost inaccessible domains, and finds security in the inhospitable regions of the north. Prussia and all the German Powers yield, as they had yielded before, to superior force, and all the lesser nations bow before the stupendous might of France.

Liberty flies aghast at the conqueror's approach, scorning the sacrifices offered up in her name, and content to bide the day of her resuscitation when tyranny should at last finally succumb to her now retarded, but nevertheless ultimately resistless advance.

Long and fierce, however, were the struggles before the supremacy of France was fairly established. Fight succeeded fight, battle succeeded battle, and slaughter followed slaughter; and many a sanguinary field, where the blood of the victor, together with that of the vanquished, flowed like water, attested the might of the combatants and the desperate nature of the struggle. But it terminated at last, and all the Continent of Europe lay prostrate at the feet of the wonderful man who controlled the destinies of France.

And in my dream I looked into times past, and saw, some fifty years ago, (about the time when the foundation of those gigantic docks were laid) the same scene enacted, by the same power, led on by the same clever and ambitious family. And methought that the mighty man who in those days had kept the world in awe, had been permitted to cast his mantle upon his successor, for good or for evil.

But there was one little spot on the map of Europe, not on the Continent, but a little island, where the Imperial flag of France did not float, and where the ruler of France had no authority. An animal of greater strength and courage than the aspiring and proud Eagle, claimed fealty of that little spot.

That animal was the British Lion, that little spot was the British Islands.

And in my dream I again recurred to years gone by, when all the Powers of Europe had been bonded together against that little spot, and all the nations of the Continent had been united under the greatest genius of the age, in order to subvert her power, and obliterate her very name from the map of the world. I saw, about the commencement of this present century, when the heights of Boulogne teemed with countless hosts of armed men destined for the conquest of that little island.

But those hosts were gathered together in vain, and that great chief, victorious over every other power, failed against this.

And why did he fail? Because here was the land of liberty, and the home of the free. With a full confidence in the goodness of her cause and a bright faith in the God of battles, that small nation had stood unmoved against a world in arms, and in the same trust is ready when necessity calls to brave it again.

And I saw in my dream, that same harbour of Cherbourg where such mighty doings had taken place in the days when the peaceful Queen of England went to visit the warlike Emperor of France; but how changed was its appearance. There was no longer any show of merry making, those splendid ships were no longer dressed in holiday garb, and their crews wore no longer the air of holiday men, and the scene had no longer a festive appearance at all. The pomp and circumstance of glorious war were there, ready to enact their stern realities, and the warlike hosts of France were gathering together, and arming for the battle against some mighty foe. Where could these vast armaments be destined for? who was there to conquer now? All Europe owned a passive obedience to the ruler of France, and who was there to dispute his almost universal sway.

It was that little spot of England that stood in the way of the conqueror, and he was now preparing to pour his numberless hosts in deluge force upon the shores of the British Isles.

At length this mighty armament leaves its moorings, and moving slowly but majestically out of the harbour, defiles upon the open sea in such seeming force and pride, as if no power on earth could possibly abide the might of its assaults; for all that art and science could possibly do to make that power irresistible, had been done.

Proudly on it moves, and sweeps over the waves, as it prepares to crush in one tremendous onslaught its last but deadly enemy, and the only one that now stands between it and universal dominion. Onward, and onward sails the gigantic host. Leaving the coast of France behind, it comes at last in sight of the devoted island.

Its shores are now plainly discernable, but those shores are alive, alive with hosts of men, men that have thrown aside for the nonce the pen and the plough, and clothed in the panoply of war with unsheathed sword and bristling cannon, silently but dauntlessly await the approach of the coming storm. Men whose hearts beat high to meet their ancient foemen in the field; men who relying on the justness of their cause, and not vainly boasting of their own strength, are prepared to shed the last drop of their blood in defence of country, of home, of family, of religion, of freedom, and of principle. But ere those shores were reached, there was a dark object seen on the waters that still interposed its vast bulk between the doomed coast and the invading squadron. A long dark line it was, spread out in bold relief against the waters, and that line must be forced ere the invader should step on the free shores of Old England, unsullied by hostile foot for eight hundred years. That line was the Wooden Walls of Old England. Long had Great Britain been called the mistress of the seas, and very justly so; for more than once her proud fleets had sailed the wide world o'er, without finding any to dispute its power, having swept all its enemies from the face of the ocean.

But her sovereignty was now disputed, and many there were of Britain's sons who thought that her supremacy on the seas could be no longer maintained, and that the sun of Albion's glory was set, that she was at last overmatched on her own element, and that now was the day of her humiliation fast approaching.

The Lion at bay is a dangerous animal. And there stood the British Lion on his metal, with mane erect, eye balls glaring, and courage roused to the uttermost, prepared to fight to the last drop of his blood. And not tamely did he wait, but only watching till his enemy was fairly within his reach, he took his deadly spring upon his advancing foe. And now the mighty hosts approach each other. The proud Lion and the haughty Eagle gathering their forces together meet in mid ocean.

Mighty was the crash of that meeting, and terrific was the conflict, when the two greatest nations of the earth awoke their dormant thunders, and rushed to the death struggle.

The very elements stood aghast, and all nature shrunk affrighted at that awful spectacle.

Faster and faster flashed the cannon's fire, louder and louder roared their dreadful thunders, and the battle raged with awful fury. But not so fast did those cannons flash, or so loud did they roar as the evil will of the angry men who worked these death-dealing engines, whose passions now roused to demoniacal fury, and bent on the destruction of their fellow-men, raged like the pent up volcano, and threatened universal destruction. One side were men fighting at the beck of an ambitious man, and sacrificing their lives to gratify his lust for universal dominion; and on the other side, they fought in the sacred cause of liberty and home.

And who should conquer in this desperate strife? "Thrice is he armed that hath his quarrel just," says the greatest of our English poets. And which must be the just cause, when liberty and freedom are pitted against the cause of despotism?

And the battle waged fiercer and fiercer, and the messengers of death flew faster and faster, and men's passions waxed hotter and hotter.

The day wore on, and still the fight raged with unabated fury. But such carnage cannot continue, or annihilation must be the result.

At length that terrible day began to wane. Still the demon raged, but his fury was also fast failing, and at last the contest draws to a close, and night fell around the contending hosts.

How stood the battle then?

I thought in my dream, that the dense clouds of smoke gradually rolled away, and the cannon's roar, and the cannon's flash grew fainter until at last they ceased. . . . . The battle was over!

And by the dim twilight I saw, oh! what a scene was there. The British Lion still waved o'er that scene, though not proudly, but in sadness it seemed to float; for it was a scene of blood and of woe. How many gallant barques were lost, how many lay shattered and helpless on the ocean, and how many brave hearts had ceased to beat. The sea was strewn with wrecks and the dead bodies of many of England's and Gallia's bravest sons, and the ocean ran red with the blood of men.

And where was now the proud Imperial Eagle? No longer soaring in its airy flight, no longer winging its unchecked course o'er the world at large; but crippled, crest-fallen and dejected it lay beneath the paws of the well nigh exhausted Lion. In the heighth of its glory, in the zenith of its power, in the day of its pride it had bearded the Lion in his den, and the enraged animal roused so rudely from his lair, had awoke his strength to the battle, and with crushing force had hurled back his daring assailant.

Of all the mighty navy that had left that great port so full of confidence, how few ships returned. The islanders were victorious. Their ancient prowess had not failed them in the day of their need, and they had maintained their ocean supremacy.

But what a victory. The enemy was repelled, the fear of invasion was past, and hostile foot had not sullied that fair soil. But the land was filled with lamentation and woe.

*   *   *   *

As I gazed on this horrible scene I shrunk with affright, and with a cry of agony I awoke from my reverie. Happy was the waking. It was all a dream, and no reality in that dreadful picture. The calm moon had risen on the sea, and was shedding her soft and mellow light on the surrounding rocks, and clothing the hill tops with silvery fire. All was peaceful. No sound of contending armies, no sea strewn with wrecks and the dead bodies of men, no lamentations and woe, but an universal air of serenity reigned around me. And may it ever continue so, thought I to myself. May the rude hand of war never disturb those peaceful valleys and verdant fields, or tinge the ocean with man's blood; may the hostile contention of monarchs no longer retard the grand march of intellect and civilisation, and may the nations cease to delight in war.

But the wish was father to the thought, for as I sat in contemplative mood o'er my reverie, methought me heard even then, the sounds of gathering hosts borne upon the winds of a not very distant future; methought the political horizon was already blackening with the accumulation of angry clouds, and that the storm that I had seen in my dream loomed dark and bloody in prospective.

And I thought to myself. What a frightful thing is war! Oh! that the vain glorious and ambitious men who indulge in war, and are the cause of it, only to gratify their lust for conquest or their love of glory; who dare to rouse the devil in men's mind, and rob him of the Angel spirit which his God has mercifully endowed him with; who transform for the time this man, created in the image of his Maker, into a being little better than a fiend, and make him play the part of licensed murderer under the sacred name of patriot, or in the sacred cause of liberty; who convert everything that is lovely and beautiful in nature into all that is hideous and unsightly, turning the most luxuriant gardens and the purest streams into arid deserts and ensanguined rivers. Oh! that these men were compelled to contemplate that wreck of humanity, that defacement of God's image, that destruction of their fellows which crowd the battle-field, the field of glory, when the fight is won. Oh! that they might be made to watch the agonies of the wounded and the dying, that they might be compelled to gaze on the distorted limbs and anguish-marked brows too plainly delineated in the forms of the dead; that they might be forced to behold the sufferings, the grief, the misery of the fatherless and the widow; that they might be made for a time to walk the earth in full view of all the desolation they have caused; that the dead, the dying, the starving, the fatherless and the broken-hearted might pass before them in ceaseless review; and that in that hour their hearts might be made of penetrable stuff, for then must they rend at such a sight, then should they melt at the rivers of blood they have shed, and the rivers of tears they have caused to flow, and war should cease from their thoughts.

But, alas, this cannot be while men are blinded by passion, and the profession of war is only regarded in holiday colours. But the day will come, perhaps not very far distant, when the love of man for his fellows shall predominate over the love of war, when the bright banners of civilisation and Christianity, led on perhaps by the glorious Anglo-Saxon race, shall be planted in all lands, and float with undisturbed majesty o'er all the universe. Then shall war cease throughout the earth.

And yet in my reverie as I thought of peace, my mind pondered on, and I resolved that in order to ensure that peace how necessary it would be to be always prepared for war, until that happy day of universal brotherhood shall arrive. I thought how much it behoved Great Britain always to be ready to assert her proper position, always to be ready to demand her place in the van of civilisation and enlightenment, and ever to be prepared at the first call of danger to that glorious edifice of freedom and liberty, that she has had so great a hand in rearing throughout the world, to defend the sacred cause to the last drop of her blood.*

Here ended Mr. Hobbler's meditations on the fêtes at Cherbourg.

The day after the opening of the Cherbourg docks, it was known in Jersey that the Atlantic Telegraph had been successfully laid, and that the happy consummation of this long talked of scheme had been announced to Her Majesty of England, even while the thunders of Cherbourg were ringing in her ears; a small steamer having sailed into that harbour during the very midst of the ceremony, as if to contrast its peace-giving news with the mighty pomp and circumstance of glorious war which were there enacting. Aye, and this little vessel was fraught with more importance for the future benefit of the world than all that gorgeous pageantry, for it sailed under the glorious

* The above visions of war were written soon after the 1st January, 1859, when the Austrian ambassador had been openly insulted by the Emperor of the French at a grand reception at the Tuileries. Since then, war has raged between the two powers, and Austria has bent beneath the power of France. Thus has a part of the drama that Hobbler saw in his dream been played out. That the remainder may never be enacted is the sincere prayer of the dreamy traveller and his editor.

banner of universal civilisation, whilst all these warlike preparations and mighty works, though necessary perhaps, so far as defensive operations are concerned, are but at best the remnants of a barbarous age. And here again was food for thought for our musing traveller, and so he mused again.

He fancied he saw the two great Continents of Europe and America brought into immediate communication with each other, and all the ends of the world united in one bond of fellowship.

The fêtes at Cherbourg appeared to pale before the accomplishment of this great work, which seemed destined to carry the blessings of civilization and christianity throughout all the Universe; to be alike instructor of the poor untutored savage of North America, as well as the better educated, but morally and religiously ignorant inhabitant of the East, and that its fire-flashing messages should carry on their lightning wings peace and good-will to all men.

But alas for man's foresight, the telegraph after all was a failure, and for the present the warlike works of Cherbourg have succeeded, while those of the peace-promoting telegraph have failed, and our hero's musings turned out as usual nothing but a myth. We still, however, most sincerely trust, that it is but hope deferred, and that ere long we shall have the glorious satisfaction of being within reach of instantaneous communication with our brethren on the other side of the Atlantic.

Wonders never cease. Hobbler, during his stay in Jersey, witnessed the appearance of one of those great luminous bodies, that in days of yore were wont to fright the world from its propriety.

He saw, and all the world saw a comet. And this comet was one that the wiseacres had said was to burn up this poor insignificant globe of ours, or if not so, it was at any rate by a switch of its gigantic tail (millions of times larger than its plaything) to have kicked the poor little earth clean out of the solar system, so that for ever after to the end of time, it was to have been tumbling about in the profound depths of unfathomable space. Yes he saw this comet, and millions of others saw this comet, and the wiseacres saw it too.

Long it lasted, and nightly charmed and delighted the dwellers upon earth with its wonderful displays of brilliancy and magnitude, and at length disappeared, and the poor little earth is not rambling about in endless space, but still rotates on its own axis, and still revolves round the great light and heat-giving orb of day. We have not even been suffocated as some would have it we were to be, for this great luminous and vapoury mass kept the most respectful distance of something like four hundred millions of miles. And this was about the last of the wondrous things our traveller saw during his trip, for the season was now fast waning.

The summer was past, and all its beautiful flowers had faded, and all its cheering sunshines were gone. Autumn, too, was well nigh spent, and he had seen the fields ripe unto the harvest, bend beneath the reapers' sickle, or the mowers' scythe. A most abundant harvest it had been too, and the extraordinarily fine season of 1858, will not very soon be forgotten.

There was a tent erected in front of the hotel for the accommodation of pic-nic and other parties. He had seen it put up at the beginning of the season, and had helped to take it down at the end of it, for the pic-nics were all defunct, and the general visitors had pretty well all returned to

England; and the season had arrived "when the swallows homewards fly," and the wingy tribes of air migrate in search of warmer climates. Our traveller, too, now began to think that it was time to hie him home to his native land.

And winter was drawing on apace, so Hobbler was forcibly reminded that the Northern shores of an island, even though so much South of London, was no longer a place for a man with delicate lungs and an impaired constitution. This he had been told long since, but he had been unable to bear the journey, for he had been very ill for some weeks past. But he had been nursed, and that right kindly, by the female members of the family. My dear reader, do you not think that the softer sex make much better nurses than the lords of Creation? I am sure Hobbler thought so, and so do I, for he never found himself so well tended by the masculine, as by the feminine species of mankind. Men may be very kind and attentive, and very strong, and do all in their power to relieve the sufferings of their patient; but they are not constituted for the display of those gentle, kindly sympathising attentions, which it comes so natural to a woman to perform. Witness the good effects produced in the sick room by that amiable and excellent lady whose presence illumined those terrible dwellings of the sick and the dying at Scutari, whose judicious and successful nursing tended so much to alleviate the bodily sufferings of the wounded and sick soldier, and whose kindly and wholesome words did so much to soothe his aching heart. All honour be to that bright and unselfish being who risked so much, endured so much, and performed so much, for the alleviation and amelioration of the condition of the suffering soldiers and sailors, the victims of a deadly war, and a deadly climate. As long as the Crimean war finds an historian to chronicle its deeds of valour, and its misdeeds of disaster—so long will there ever be found one to speak of that bold, devoted, heroic woman Florence Nightingale, who relinquished rank, wealth and comfort, for the hard, but to her delightful, task of sharing in the sufferings of her fellow countrymen. But it is not for me to sing the praises of this excellent lady, they have been chanted by hundreds and thousands of tongues far more eloquent than mine, but still I may be allowed to add my mite to the vast treasury of those praises.

But to return to my subject. Hobbler was kindly nursed, and Hobbler liked female society. He does not attempt to deny it, for he perfectly agrees with a remark he saw in the leading London journal "that without female society man becomes brutish."

The fern cutting was over, and the autumnal vraic gathering had taken place; the hills looked bleak and naked, the sun began to assume a watery appearance, the evenings were damp and chilly, and winter every where proclaimed his near approach. A word or two about this fern cutting and vraic gathering, and their uses.

The fern when cut, is dried and gathered together in bundles and stored away for the winter, as litter for the cattle. The sea-weed forms not only the principal manure of the island, but is also used as fuel. Some farmers spread it on their land in its natural state, as it is gathered from the shore; but others use it as fuel first, and then spread the ashes over the land. There are some very curious laws about this fern cutting and vraic gathering. Nobody is allowed to cut the one or gather the other until a stated day, and then only between sunrise and sunset.

The seigneurs of the Manors have some especial privileges as regards the sea-weed, being allowed several hours start of the ordinary people. The weed which is gathered from the neighbouring rocks, or collected from the driftings on shore, is spread out upon the beach to dry, and it is somewhat curious to see the rigid principles of honour with which each person's lot of weed is guarded. At this employment, the women work even harder than the men, and you may often see them ascending the rocks with large bundles of vraic on their shoulders—and rocks, too, whose sides are so precipitous that the generality of people would hardly care to climb them without any incumbrance.

I had almost forgotten to introduce my readers to one of the principle features of this pretty spot; but the fact is that Hobbler was so taken up with the Bouley Hotel and its amusements, or its labours, whichever you please, that he had well nigh omitted it altogether. And when I come to inform my readers what his short comings of memory really are, I am not satisfied that they will be content with any apology or explanation he can make for them. So according to my advice, he pleads guilty, and humbly craves your mercy, kind reader, acknowledging that he ought to be..... but no matter what; he is deeply penitent for his breach of gallantry (for such it is) and hastens to make all the amends in his power by immediately ushering you into the presence of the Ladies of Bouley.

Yes, this neglected object, is a group of ladies, and ladies of high character, too ; for these ladies of Bouley, that he has hitherto so shamefully slighted, are ladies of the most unimpeachable character, of a most elevated position in the world, the observed of all observers, soaring high above the sublunary things of this earth, yet at the same time ladies who are most innocent in their manners, and most simple in their habits; finding in the birds of the air their companions, and foreswearing all the pleasures, as well as scorning the dwellings of men, taking shelter only beneath the canopy of heaven ; making the rocks their dwelling place, and subsisting upon the pure dews that descend from the skies, or the mists that arise from earth. They are most retiring in their dispositions, often veiling their fair forms in the clouds and vapours that hover o'er this nether world ; and yet they are ever to be found at their posts, for they may be seen kissing the early mists of rising dawn, and welcoming the lark as he rises at break of day and soars on his heavenward course; at scorching noontide they may be found basking in the meridian sun, and later in the day they are still visible, as they lave their fair persons in the dewy twilight of evening.

This bevy of fair ones consists, however, of only two persons, an elderly lady and a young damsel. The matron, who is supposed to be far advanced in years, is always to be observed in a sitting posture, never having been seen by anybody in an erect position, and as far as our traveller could learn from personal observation, was rather of a studious turn of mind, and probably a literary character (though we much doubt if she ever attempted to write a book) for she was never to be found without a volume in her hand, upon which she appeared to be intently occupied. She always appears in public, as perhaps it were well all elderly ladies should appear, with covered head; wearing a bonnet at all times, aye, and a real bonnet too, not a top knot apology of modern times, but a good old fashioned bonnet of the coal scuttle shape. Of the old lady's beauty, or general personal appearance, Hobbler could not say much, as from the peculiar position in which she always sits, it is impossible to form an opinion.

The maiden appears from her figure to be young and rather graceful, and of a remarkably modest and pensive disposition; her face and figure being hidden by a veil, and her body always in a leaning and contemplative attitude. The proper time to see this fair damsel to advantage, is when the sun is mellowing surrounding nature with the golden tints of his departing glory; for this young lady is so modest, that she likes not the glaring light of noonday, but exhibits her charms only in the soft and retiring light of evening.

Such are the Ladies of Bouley. Allow me then to introduce you, my dear reader. Mr. — or Mrs. —, the Ladies of Bouley—The Ladies of Bouley, Mr. — or Mrs.—. You make your bow to the ladies, but they move not; you offer your salutations, but they do not reply; they neither heed your speech, nor attend to your genuflexions. Your politeness is unreturned, for they know no politeness, they study no manners; stiff, dumb and unbending, they care nought about you.

And why? Because they are but nature's freaks in rock-work, a sort of elemental carving on the face of the craggy cliffs, a little game that the winds and the atmosphere have played off on the rocks of Bouley. And so Boreas & Co. have turned sculptors. Behold their work in these two figures, which are, however, joking apart, very curious—especially the representation of the young lady, which when viewed from the pier at sundown, or a little before, has the appearance of being clothed in a beautifully fine veil, through which the head and body are plainly discernable, and much reminds one of the celebrated veiled figure by Monti in the Austrian department of the Great Exhibition of 1851. Like all naturally formed figures in rock or chalk, these are found to be nothing but rough unshapen masses on a close inspection.

October is chanting his own last dying lays, and the chill fogs of November are preparing to sing his requiem, and our traveller sets to work in earnest to pack up his traps and curiosities. The latter were soon done, only consisting of a few shells and sea-weeds, and such like things generally found on the sea-shore. The former he was not troubled about, having fallen into such good hands, that all those little matters were done for him.

"Happy man!" some of you will exclaim, "who would not like to be an invalid to be waited on in this manner?" Halt a moment, my kind friends. To be nursed, and petted, and coddled, if you like the word, as he was, you must be a sick man, and I would ask any of you seriously whether you would undergo the ordeal for the sake of the reward.

Beyond doubt it is worth while to endure a great deal of suffering, for the sake of receiving those kind attentions that the sick man is always certain to meet with at the hands of the softer sex, and upon which we have already expatiated. But query, how much suffering would you, reader, (of course at this moment I appeal to the male portion of my readers) undergo to receive a like amount of kindness. Our traveller had been invalided, crippled, and even condemned by the doctors for more than two years, and though I do not say he was entitled to all the kindnesses he received wherever he went, and for which he was most deeply grateful, still I think his comparatively helpless condition went far to ensure it for him, from all warm and charitable hearts. But the luggage is all packed, and our traveller's last evening at Bouley has arrived, and wishing all his friends adieu, he retired to bed.

Before closing this Chapter, our traveller would wish to say a word or two about the treatment he received at this Bouley Bay hotel.

Upwards of four months he had been located in that pleasant house by the lone sea-shore, and when he quitted it, it was with feelings of great regret. For four months he had received the most unremitting kindness and attention from every one in the house, and he would here wish to bear his grateful testimony to their general and uniform kindness, assiduity, and attention, not only to himself, but also to all comers to their hotel.

Reader, in concluding this Chapter, if ever you go to Jersey, (and if you wish to see pretty scenery go there by all means) let me advise you to pay a visit to Bouley; and if you are able to procure accommodation at the hotel there, I feel confident from our traveller's description of it, that you will be charmed by the scenery with which it is surrounded, delighted with its daily life and evening solitude, and you cannot fail to be pleased and satisfied with the treatment you receive there. Should you go, fail not to mention when you arrive there, that you come at the recommendation of the " lame man of Bouley."

CHAPTER VII.

HOMEWARD BOUND.

Departure from Bouley.—Day-break.—Beautiful effects.—Adieu to Jersey.—A November day on board a Steamer.—Little episode on the Voyage.—Cupid and Uniforms.—The Guard's Story about the Livery.—Arrival at Southampton.--Hobbler on the Custom-house.—The Author's Adieu to the Reader.

To rise with the lark is early work, but to rise before the lark, when all nature is steeped in the gloom of night is extraordinarily early work, and proves the man who does it to be, in the getting up way, an extraordinary man.

Well such was the case with Hobbler. On a cold, cheerless November morning he rose from his bed somewhere about half past four, long before chanticleer had even proclaimed the approach of dawn. The greater part of the household were fast in the arms of Morpheus when he made his appearance below stairs all equipped for his long journey. Bidding his host good bye, he hobbled into his cab and finally quitted his Jersey home about half past five. 'Twas in the night that Hobbler quitted this home, but the moon was shining brightly, and ere he had reached the top of the hill, the day began to dawn.

> " Upon the hill he turned,
> To take a last fond look,
> Of the valley,'' and the rocky shore,
> And his dwelling by the brook.

Who that has travelled through the night, or watched by a sick bed, or lain on a bed of sickness himself, but has seen and watched the breaking of the day; how like a little speck of light bursting from out its night-shroud it first appears in the eastern horizon, then little by little it spreads over the heavens, the night clouds roll gradually away, the stars fade, and the silvery moon pales before the approach of morning's dawn.

So it was on the morning of Hobbler's departure from Bouley, as from the top of the hill he watched the fair Aurora leap forth into new life.

The earth began to lose its deep shadows,

object after object came into view, rock after rock, hill after hill became visible, and at last even the far off coast of France loomed thick in its distant and misty morning garb. The sea lost its heaviness, and again resumed its transparent hue, a beautiful violet tint spread over the earth, and sea and sky seemed to combine in that early morning scene; and finally the old hotel at the bottom of the hill crept out from her shadowy retreat beneath the fern-clad hills, and stood out in bold relief against the gorgeous crimson and purple tints of the heavens, which spread themselves over the eastern sky, and proclaimed the approach of day's great ruler.

> " But yonder comes the powerful king of day,
> Rejoicing in the east, the lessening cloud,
> The kindling azure. and the mountain's brow
> Illum'd with fluid gold, his near approach
> Betoken glad."

The brow of the hill is now reached, and so farewell to thee old Bouley. St. Heliers and its harbours are attained ere the sun has shaken off his misty robe, the steam of the mail packet Courier is up, and she lies at the pier head ready to convey our traveller back to the land of his birth.

There were some friends waiting to see him off, but long leave takings are not pleasant things, and wishing all of them good bye, he stepped on board the packet.

At half past seven she steamed out of port, and with kissing of hands, and waving of handkerchiefs, and all the little affecting et ceteras that must naturally occur when parting with friends with whom you have spent months in close and social intercourse, and whom you may never see again, Hobbler bade adieu to Jersey.

Soon after quitting it, Serk hove in sight, and then Guernsey, which latter island was reached about ten o'clock. Before leaving St. Heliers, our traveller had been congratulated on the fineness and calmness of the morning, but it turned out to be a day of quite the reverse character. The wind which had been blowing hard all night, had only moderated for a short time, and before reaching Guernsey it had again become very boisterous, and the sun which had only made its appearance for a few minutes, was now completely hidden by dark lowering clouds.

Ere long it began to rain a sort of Scotch mist, and the wind came in fitful gusts, dashing the spray over the vessel at the rise of almost every wave, and the day became altogether one of a very unpleasant character.

Alderney and the Caskets were passed about midday, and soon after, owing to the haziness of the weather, were lost sight of altogether.

The wind being right a-head, and the vessel being very heavily laden with cattle and general merchandise, her progress was not very rapid. The atmosphere, too, was cold and raw, and our hero not being able to move about, the voyage became very tedious.

About three o'clock in the afternoon, the captain and the mate stationed themselves on the bridge to look out for land, but they had to look a monstrous long while before they found it, much to the annoyance of the poor sick folk on board; for the majority of the passengers had already succumbed either to the pitching of the vessel, or to the unpleasant effluvia that is always to be met with on board a steamer, especially in thick weather, when the steam and smoke, and smell of grease are continually driven down upon deck.

The cabin, on such occasions, not being at all a pleasant place, our traveller was obliged to content himself with sitting still upon the deck. He was well wrapped up in a thick overcoat, and as the sea washed occasionally over him, he could not help coming to the conclusion, that his coat was being converted into a perpetual barometer, and his face undergoing a slow but sure process of pickling. But this tedious day wore on, and it was not altogether unrelieved by amusement. Among the sick folk on board was a young lady, who having borne up against adverse circumstances for a long while, was obliged at last to give way, and became in such an hysterical state, that the mate and some of the passengers were quite alarmed about her, and the stewardess was most unremitting in her attentions, applying all sorts of sedatives and restoratives to try and alleviate her sufferings. But old Dame Nature was after all the best nurse, and the sight of a rather dashing young officer of her Majesty's army was the best restorative. The former recommended sleep, which was accepted and proved beneficial; the latter recommended himself, and was also accepted, and to judge by the merry ringing laugh of this lately half dying and hysterical young lady, his company must have also been highly beneficial. Indeed, there was but little left in that merry face of the ghostly appearance that she had presented but a short time before, and the presence of the gallant son of Mars acted like a powerful elixir, and to judge from all appearances it was not very far removed from the elixir of love.

In the early part of the day she had engrossed all the attentions of the stewardess, they were now dispensed with, and she engrossed all those of this gallant gay Lothario, who, in his turn, certainly monopolised all the ideas of the young lady. I might describe this couple if I thought it would be edifying to my readers, but as I am extremely doubtful on that point, I will leave it alone, especially as I presume that few people ever travel without witnessing some such scene. Suffice it to say, that our traveller confesses to having been amused for all the rest of his voyage with this flirtation, which was doubtless one of those little scenes that are always sure to occur when highly excitable young ladies are thrown into the company of dashing young officers; for depend upon it, in such cases, the artful little god who has always a spare arrow in his quiver, and who rarely misses his aim, is sure to strike full home. There is in such a case no resisting the charms of the livery.

Oh! this livery—uniform—if you like it better, my particular reader, what a deal it has to answer for. Perhaps it would not be altogether out of place to introduce an anecdote respecting "the livery," that came under the notice of the author some few years ago.

He was riding behind the mail coach from London to Dover, and having entered into conversation with the guard, found him a very pleasant and jolly fellow. By the bye, perhaps some of my elder readers who recollect the mail coaches in their prime, will say that it was not customary for passengers to travel with the guard at all. Exactly so, but somehow or other with the day mails (and this was a day mail I am speaking of) they were not so particular, and the coach being full in front, I was accommodated with a seat at the back.

But to my story. The guard was not the handsomest man in the world, indeed he was what some people would call rather ugly, and others very ugly; a sort of square cut visage with a few hairs dibbed into his head and face, eyes rather fishy, and a nose, the end of which always pointed heavenward; but he was very good tempered, and this appeared in his face. The day was not a pleasant one, much such another as the one Hobbler was now spending on board the Jersey homeward-bound packet. So our guard put on his great coat, a very seedy sort of an affair. It had once been brown, I should think, but it was impossible to say, for it was such a venerable coat, covered with successive layers of the dirt of ages, and the dust of many roads. It was now indeed a coat of many colours, and I should add it was his own private property, and consequently not his official coat.

Early in the afternoon the coach approached Canterbury, by that pretty road which all who have ever visited that city must remember, called Harbledown Hill, which commands a fine view of the venerable cathedral, and all the adjacent town and country.

No sooner had we come in sight of this city than our guard, to my astonishment, took off his great coat, though it was still raining fast, and pulling a small piece of looking glass out of his pocket began combing his hairs. I believe it is usual to speak in the singular number of the hairy covering of the head, but in this case I call them hairs, for they were so very scanty you might almost have counted them. Seeing my look of astonishment, my worthy friend looked up with an enquiring glance to know what I could possibly be surprised at. " What are you up to?" I exclaimed, " You surely do not think that any of the girls in Canterbury will be looking after such an ugly fellow as you." He laughed at my innocence. A sort of merry, contemptuous laugh, to think that I should be so green. It is true, I was but very young at the time.

Taking another look in the glass at his ugly but good tempered face, and having another rake at the stray hairs, and appearing to be perfectly satisfied in his own mind that he was a plain man, he looked up at me, and with a waggish expression, he tapped with his fingers his beautiful new red official coat, which he now displayed in all its glory, and said, " It is the livery, Sir, that does it." And then he sat himself down, and blowing a defiant charge on his bugle, seemed to fancy himself some old Roman warrior, seated in his triumphal car. And I must candidly confess that the livery did do it, for after we had passed through the city, as he drew on his time honoured garment, and again consigned his brilliant uniform to obscurity, he turned to me with the same knowing smile and said, " Well, Sir, and what do you think of the livery now?" I could only allow that he was right about it, and that I was exceedingly green on the subject. I don't think I have ever been so since; as that day, I certainly learnt my first lesson of its value. All the way through the streets, the bright scarlet uniform was a very great source of attraction, and many a young girl, aye, and many a pretty one too, had returned with a good humoured nod the friendly salutation of our ugly guard; and I had almost wished I was a guard myself.

Yes, *the livery* is all powerful it must be owned, whether it be the livery of the cloth which is exceedingly attractive now adays, or her Majesty's livery of red, blue or green, or the exceedingly popular and varied liveries of the rifle corps; or in other ranks, the railway livery and many others, to say nothing of the official garb of flunkeyism, all in their own peculiar sphere have their attractions, perhaps too much so, and therefore the old guard was right, " that the livery does it."

Your pardon, kind reader, for this digression.

To return to the steam boat and Hobbler. Night began to creep on, and the captain and the mate were still looking out for the land they could not find. Their search was, however, at last rewarded by the sudden appearance of a red light, looking gloomy and grand through the gathering mists of evening. This proved to be the Needles Lighthouse, and soon after the vessel entered the Solent and smooth water. What a change then took place on board that ship. The poor sick people began to look up, and the colour returned to some of their cheeks; the attentions of the steward and stewardess were dispensed with, at least as far as they might be regarded in the light of sick nurses, some of the more valiant of the male passengers were bold enough to light up cigars, our lovers walked the deck with all the confidence of a promenade at the Crystal Palace on Saturdays, and before long the majority were engaged in discussing a leg of mutton and trimmings. As we entered the Solent, the Needles looked like grim old sentinels, and the Isle of Wight lay an undistinguishable black mass upon the ocean, except when illumined by some blue lights that were let off to tell the folks at the telegraph station at Hurst Point that we had escaped the dangers of the Channel. The vessel pokes her way on in the dark, and before nine o'clock it entered Southampton docks, and our traveller after passing through the fiery ordeal of the Custom House, found himself sitting soon after that hour before a blazing fire in the coffee room of an hotel in that town. And right glad was he to sit before that fire, for he found himself upon his arrival in England, also arrived in midwinter, which had set in uncommonly early, and very severe. And as he sat by the fire-side, he thought of the scenes he had just witnessed at the Custom House, and as he thought the musing fit came upon him, and this was the last of his musings:—

HOBBLER ON THE CUSTOM-HOUSE.

What a horrid thing is that Custom House, and what a complicated piece of machinery it is, very marvellous no doubt in its ramifications but exceedingly unpleasant in its workings. It contributes very largely to the revenue of the country but then it pries so into all one's little secret purchases, and exposes one's wardrobe in such an unseemly manner to the public gaze, no matter whether it be handsome or shabby. If the former, perhaps, it does not so much matter; but if the latter, who is there that is anxious for such a display? It is moreover so very annoying, that one cannot indulge in a little quiet cheat if one likes, when it is only at the expense of the country. To think that any one of the fair sex especially, should be subjected to such indignities; her luggage overhauled, her garments rudely handled, her trinkets inspected, and to fill up the measure of the annoyance, sundry little articles of foreign manufacture cleverly concealed (though not cleverly enough to escape the lynx eyes of these terrible land-sharks) in the luggage, ruthlessly abstracted by these rude officials, and still more ruthlessly confiscated by the state, of which these officials are the representatives. If a lady is so inclined, why may she not practice a little sleight of hand? By all means, if she can ensure success, and quiet her conscience for committing what must be called, though perhaps harshly, a fraud upon the country; for what the legislators of a free country like England have fixed upon as the necessary dues to be enforced, as requisite for the support of its laws and position, must either be paid, or the country's government cannot be carried on; and therefore any evasion of those dues cannot be designated by any less harsh word than a fraud practised upon one's country, especially when it is considered that the parties making those laws are supposed to be elected by the voice of the people at large

Of course these remarks apply to the men as well as the fair sex; though when the former indulge in smuggling, it is generally on a larger scale, and it must be confessed that it is the ladies who are generally the victims of the rough treatment that I now so much deplored, and which I was discussing in my mind as I sat before the fire. Did these ladies ever think of what they were doing, or what indignities they were subjecting themselves to? Far be it from any chivalrous man, and my editor has already told the reader that I am one, to stand up and maintain the cause of the ladies against all comers; far be it, I say, from any chivalrous man to say that they do it from the love of cheating, such an idea can never enter their heads by any possibility, though they do perhaps prize the article a little more because it comes somewhat cheaper than they can procure it in England, but then they prize it a great deal more from the idea that they have outwitted the cunning Jack-in-office. And as I thought of the rudeness that I had seen some of the ladies subjected to that day, I mused on, and wondered when the day would come that they should no longer be liable to such treatment; when all those articles of virtu, and pretty little things of foreign manufacture, to say nothing of articles of dress, and delicious scents which are so temptingly displayed in the shops of Paris, and other Continental cities, might be openly exposed in their luggage, instead of being hidden; or when concealment would no longer be necessary, and when the day would arrive that those rude officers should be placed on the shelf, as no longer of any use, or be put under a glass case and exhibited in some national museum, as one of the wonders of bye gone days.

Free trade in one country, and not in another, is at best a very imperfect system; but the days will perhaps come when free trade notions shall be universal, and when the wishes and efforts of England to extend it to all her imports may be reciprocated by every other nation. Then could Great Britain find in the increase of her manufactures and consequent increase of her excisable revenue, an equivalent for the loss of her customs' duties; and then and not till then could the hateful Custom House with all its uses and all its abuses be abolished; and all its dark deeds of insult, oppression, abstraction, and confiscation might be chronicled in the pages of history as things that once were, but now happily no longer exist. And as I mused, I fancied I saw the arrival of that happy day, when one could land in England, the same as one lands in Jersey, without being waylaid by a hateful Custom House officer. Soon may that day arrive, when sleight of hand shall no longer be a requisite portion of a traveller's education.

And Hobbler woke up from his musings and went to bed, and the next morning started for London, where he arrived without let or hindrance.

The musings of Hobbler are ended, as well as his wanderings and his dreamings.

And now, kind reader, you, who have accompanied me thus far through this tangled mass of words, I have only to inform you that my task is finished, to solicit for the last time your pardon for having indulged in such dreamy effusions, to thank you for all your patience and forbearance, and to bid you adieu.

If I have afforded you any amusement or instruction by these writings, I am most truly pleased ; and if I have failed to do so, I can only humbly apologise for having trenched so deeply on your time. If I have created in any of you a wish to visit these Channnel Islands, by the description of their beautiful scenery, let me advise you by all means to go and judge for yourselves, feeling quite convinced that my poor feeble pen is quite inadequate to paint their beauties in colours sufficiently glowing to do them justice ; and if I have failed altogether to stir within you any such desire, be not guided by my descriptions, but only take my advice, and go there.

Go, again I repeat it, and see for yourselves, for it must be that I am very deficient in descriptive power, most certainly, it is not these islands that are deficient in anything that is beautiful in landscape scenery. And once more I would say, go.

Dark clouds hover over the political horizon, war and rumours of war are abroad, the Continent of Europe may even in this approaching summer be in a state of open warfare, at any rate it will be in a disturbed state, and travelling there be unpleasant if not dangerous. And even if this were not the case, why should you ramble so far in search of nature's beauties—why should you seek them in countries governed by despotic laws and where the traveller is subjected to so many indignities and so many impositions, when you can find them nearer home, rich and rare as the eye can wish to gaze upon, and where you will be under the protection of that flag, the bright symbol of liberty that floats over the great, the glorious and the free nation of Old England, and all those beautiful islands that own allegiance to the sovereign of Great Britain.

Reader, farewell, the Hobblings of Tom Hobbler are ended.

FINIS.

www.ingramcontent.com/pod-product-compliance
Lightning Source LLC
Chambersburg PA
CBHW021403230426
43666CB00006B/620